The Heritage Book 1995

Edna McCann

Maxwell Macmillan Canada

Maxwell Macmillan Canada
1200 Eglinton Avenue East, Suite 200
Don Mills, Ontario M3C 3N1

ISBN 02.954260-X

Printed and bound in Canada
⊛ Printed on Acid Free Paper

Nineteenth Edition

PICTURE CREDITS

As my readers know, I like to devote a good deal of time to volunteer work in my community. The hours I spend reading to young children at the local school or visiting with shut-ins at a nearby nursing home are some of my most fulfilling. It often amazes me how little it takes to make a difference in another person's life.

Writing *The Heritage Book* for the past nineteen years has connected me with an even larger community. My readers live all over North America, and it gives me great joy to visit them every day in their homes through this little book. We are all members of the human fellowship, and we all have a part to play in creating a safe and vibrant society. I hope that my collection of quotes and stories inspires you to reach out to your neighbours and make a difference in your community.

I offer you the 1995 edition of *The Heritage Book* in hopes that it may contribute in some small way to a fulfilling and happy year.

January

Our birth is but a sleep and a forgetting:
  The soul that rises with us, our life's star,
Hath had elsewhere its setting,
    And cometh from afar:
  Not in entire forgetfulness,
  And not in utter nakedness,
But trailing clouds of glory do we come
    From God, who is our home:
Heaven lies about us in our infancy!
                    —*William Wordsworth*

Every "infant" new year is a gracious gift, an opportunity to reflect on times past and look ahead with hope and fresh purpose.

THE HERITAGE BOOK

I GREET our new year with excitement, anticipation, and yes, even a little trepidation. For
as time passes I have learned that every day of
every year holds something new and interesting, if only we take the time to see and appreciate it.

I am also aware that a year's passing can
bring with it surprises. Some are good—
finding out for example that you are able to
work the computer at the library with almost
as much expertise as the cute six-year-old who
is working beside you; some are not so good—
realizing that no matter how much you would
like to deny it you need to use a hearing aid if
you are to be able to carry on any sort of
reasonable conversation with friends and
family.

It is the unknown that lends the excitement,
and occasionally the tinge of fear, to each
coming day.

I have found that the best way to stay
optimistic and happy is to simply accept what
comes—and make the best of what cannot be
changed.

THE HERITAGE BOOK

TUESDAY — JANUARY 3

IF you don't scale the mountain you can't see the view.

WEDNESDAY — JANUARY 4

SOME years ago a genius (in my opinion at least) invented stickum notes. These small, yellow pieces of paper with a sticky edge have become invaluable both in the workplace and the home.

My granddaughter Phyllis loves to write little notes and attach them to the sandwich wrappings in Jenny and Justin's lunches.

"Your hair looked beautiful this morning, Jenny, love Mom," or "Hope your team does well today Justin, love Mom."

My son-in-law Bruce often has these little notes pasted all over the work he brings home from the office.

I like to carry a pad of them in my pocket so that if I hear an interesting story or quote for my writing I just jot it down and stick the note in my writing folder.

I guess stickum notes fall into the category of "how ever did we get along without them?"

<u>THURSDAY — JANUARY 5</u>

BEFORE you give somebody a piece of your mind, make sure you can get by with what you have left.

<u>FRIDAY — JANUARY 6</u>

TODAY, the twelfth day after Christmas, is the celebration of the Epiphany. As well, many European friends will celebrate the birth of Jesus today. In tribute I offer a verse from a favourite hymn for this occasion.

As with gladness men of old
Did the guiding star behold,
As with joy they hailed its light,
Leading onward, beaming bright;
So most gracious Lord may we
Evermore be led to thee.

<u>SATURDAY — JANUARY 7</u>

IT'S not true that nice guys finish last. Nice guys are winners before the game even starts.

—*Addison Walker*

THE HERITAGE BOOK

SUNDAY — JANUARY 8

Do not judge lest you be judged yourselves. For in the way you judge, you will be judged, and by your standard of measure, it shall be measured to you.

—Matthew 7:1-2

MONDAY — JANUARY 9

In recent years my son-in-law Bruce has lost much of his hair, and while at first this caused him concern, he has come to accept the inevitable and can now enjoy "bald" humour.

He was chuckling as he came in this evening. "Mother, I want you to know there is a 'politically correct' term that describes those of us with receding hairlines. I am no longer bald, I am 'folically challenged,'" he laughed.

TUESDAY — JANUARY 10

My coat and I live comfortably together. It has assumed all my wrinkles, does not hurt me anywhere, has moulded itself on my deformities and is complacent to all my movements. I only feel its presence because it keeps me warm. Old coats are old friends.

—Victor Hugo

THE HERITAGE BOOK

<u>Wednesday — January 11</u>

My dear friend Emily writes from her winter home in warm and sunny Florida.

"You know Edna, as someone born and raised in a four-season part of the United States I often wondered what it would be like to live in an area that has only two seasons. My friend John, who has never lived anywhere but Florida, summed it up very well."

"I've always been aware of the passing of one season to another. The leaves don't change colour down here—but the licence plate colours sure do."

<u>Thursday — January 12</u>

My very dear friend Jake Frampton stopped in for dinner this evening. Jake is always good company, and because it was our first get-together since Christmas it was most enjoyable to compare our holiday seasons and interesting family stories.

Ralph Waldo Emerson said, "A friend is a person with whom I may be sincere. Before him I may think aloud."

THE HERITAGE BOOK

FRIDAY — JANUARY 13

THIS is one of those infrequent days when the thirteenth day of the month falls on a Friday, and our thoughts turn to that fateful phenomenon of luck.

A book, like a person, has its fortunes with one; is lucky or unlucky in the precise moment of its falling in our way, and often by some happy accident counts with us for something more than its independent value.

—*Walter Pater*

SATURDAY — JANUARY 14

MY friends Will and Muriel were enjoying a winter's walk when Muriel slipped on an icy patch on the sidewalk and went down heavily, giving her ankle a nasty twist.

"Oh Will, I think you'll have to carry me home," moaned Muriel.

"You're right, dear," said Will as he eyed Muriel's ample frame, "but I'm afraid I'll have to make two trips."

Laughing, Muriel was able to limp home.

SUNDAY — JANUARY 15

ONE of the first prayers that we learned is still among the loveliest.

Our Father who art in heaven, Hallowed be Thy Name, Thy Kingdom come, Thy will be done, in earth as it is in heaven. Give us this day our daily bread; And forgive us our trespasses, As we forgive those that trespass against us; And lead us not into temptation, But deliver us from evil. For Thine is the kingdom the power and the glory, forever and ever. Amen.

MONDAY — JANUARY 16

MY great-grandchildren Justin and Jenny enjoyed a visit with us this weekend.

Nine is a wonderful age for children; young enough to enjoy an occasional cuddle at night yet old enough to participate in meaningful conversations with grandparents and great-grandparents.

Suzanne Larronde put it well when she said, "The pairing of young and old creates an openness not always found in adult relationships."

THE HERITAGE BOOK

Log cabin in the country
   clad in winter's snowy cloak
Is nestled 'neath the shelter
   of a gnarled and barren oak.
Atop each standing fence post
   a snowy cap does fit,
A flash of colour lingers
   where the hardy bluejays flit.
From depths of homey cabin
   the warm lights radiate.
Outside the gate, with patience
   old Dobbin stands in wait
In harness, spit and polished,
   all hitched up to the sleigh.
The bells will ring out clearly
   folks will soon be on their way.
As they snuggle deep within the robes
   to foil the frosty air,
The muffled clop of horses' hooves
   ring out upon the air.
The crunching of the runners,
   O'er the snow so cold and white
Fades 'way to just an echo
   as the sleigh glides out of sight.

—*Margaret Jewell*

WEDNESDAY — JANUARY 18

I HAVE discovered the secret of happiness—it is work, either with the hands or the head. The moment I have something to do, the draughts are open and my chimney draws, and I am happy.

—John Burroughs

THURSDAY — JANUARY 19

CHINESE philosopher Lao-tse writes about personal qualities:

I have three things which I hold fast and prize. The first is gentleness; the second is frugality; the third is humility which keeps me from putting myself before others. Be gentle and you can be bold; be frugal and you can be liberal; avoid putting yourself before others and you can become a leader among men.

FRIDAY — JANUARY 20

LET us be thankful for the fools. But for them the rest of us could not succeed.

—Mark Twain

THE HERITAGE BOOK

Ten Commandments For Good Living

1. Speak to people: there is nothing so nice as a cheerful word of greeting.
2. Smile at people: it takes seventy-two muscles to frown, only fourteen to smile.
3. Call people: the sweetest music to anyone's ears is the sound of his or her own name.
4. Be friendly and helpful: if you would have friends, be a friend.
5. Be cordial: speak and act as if everything you do is a real pleasure.
6. Be genuinely interested in people—you can like almost everybody if you try.
7. Be generous with praise—cautious with criticism.
8. Be considerate with the feelings of others.
9. Give service where you can; what counts most in life is what we do for others.
10. If you have a good sense of humour, patience, and humility you will be rewarded manifold.

SUNDAY — JANUARY 22

THEN Jesus said unto them, "Truly, truly I say unto you, it is not Moses that gave you bread from heaven, it is my Father who gives you the true bread from heaven. For the bread of God is that which comes down out of heaven, and gives life to the world." They said therefore to Him, "Lord evermore give us this bread." Jesus said to them, "I am the bread of life, he who comes to me shall not hunger, and he who believes in me shall never thirst."

—John 6:32-35

MONDAY — JANUARY 23

AUTHOR William Saroyan, who died of cancer in May 1981, once wrote that "the best part" of a person "stays forever."

Shortly before his death he phoned the Associated Press to report that cancer had spread to several of his vital organs. He left with reporters his final statement to be used after his death.

"Everybody has got to die, but I have always believed an exception would be made in my case. Now what?"

THE HERITAGE BOOK

An author whose works I have enjoyed reading again and again is James Herriot, the Scottish veterinary surgeon.

Herriot grew up in Glasgow and received his training at Glasgow Veterinary College. Shortly afterwards he took the position of assistant in a practice in North Yorkshire.

His warm and witty stories of his animal patients and their wide range of owners have entertained millions of readers over the years.

You can imagine my great pleasure then when my grandson Marshall and his wife Jamie dropped in this evening with a series of cassette tapes of the complete works of James Herriot read by the author himself.

"I know how much you enjoy reading his books, Gran, but we thought that maybe you would like hearing his stories with the authentic accent."

For the past two hours I have sat enraptured, listening to the wonderful brogue of a true Scotsman telling the tales of people who feel like old friends to me.

If you have never enjoyed the pleasure of books on tapes I heartily recommend that you try it soon.

WEDNESDAY — JANUARY 25

BUT pleasures are like poppies spread—
You seize the flow'r, its bloom is shed;
Or like the snow falls in the river—
A moment white—then melts forever.

These words are from the great poet Robbie Burns on this, his birthday.

THURSDAY — JANUARY 26

NOTHING ever becomes real till it is experienced—Even a proverb is no proverb to you till your Life has illustrated it.

—John Keats

FRIDAY — JANUARY 27

THAT is happiness; to be dissolved into something complete and great.

— Willa Cather

THE HERITAGE BOOK

For the past few years my daughter Marg, her husband Bruce and I have enjoyed what seems to have become a tradition—a winter picnic.

Today the three of us chose a beautiful route heading east along the north shore of Lake Ontario.

Through Port Hope and Cobourg and on past Brighton and Trenton the scenery was spectacular. Winds off the lake had showered the branches with a sparkling layer of ice and the trees shimmered in their coats of diamond.

In Picton we savoured our lunch of steaming chicken soup from thermos jugs, biscuits with thick wedges of cheddar cheese, and lemon tea.

Several of the town's antique stores were open and we browsed leisurely, chatting with the owners who seemed pleased to have company on a cold winter's day.

The ride home was equally pleasurable, and we arrived tired but satisfied just as the stars were appearing in the night sky.

I can heartily recommend a winter picnic as an excellent and inexpensive "pick me up."

THE HERITAGE BOOK

I THE Lord will hold your right hand, saying to you, "Don't be afraid; I will help you."
—*Isaiah 41:13*

T HE rare individual who unselfishly tries to serve others has an enormous advantage. He has little competition.
—*Dale Carnegie*

N EVER lose an opportunity of seeing anything that is beautiful; for beauty is God's handwriting—a wayside sacrament. Welcome it in every fair face, in every fair sky, in every fair flower, and thank God for it as a cup of blessing.
—*Ralph Waldo Emerson*

February

Winter Night

Winter—cold is the night.
Chiseled in deepest blue,
Each star-shape silver-white
Shines cold—clear down the sky's long
  avenue.
The rich moon with its broadly streaming flood
Washes with light
The earth whereon I stand.
The icy ether fires my smouldering blood,
The stars I breathe and feel,
The magic heavens my trembling senses
  steal,
Until, exquisitely unmanned,
My spirits swoon
With the delicious cold, the dark, the riding
  moon.

—*Melville Cane*

THE HERITAGE BOOK

IN Ontario we refer to this day as "Groundhog Day." In the British Isles it is "Candlemas Day."

Whichever of the two traditions you look to it seems that we could be in for another six weeks of winter.

"Wiarton Willie," the small groundhog prodded from his hole this morning, saw his shadow. This ominous occurrence predicts more winter weather to come, as does this traditional Scottish rhyme.

If Candlemas Day be dry and fair,
The half o' winter's to come and mair;
If Candlemas Day be wet and foul,
The half o' winter's gone at Yule.

PEOPLE who have warm friends are healthier and happier than those who have none. A single real friend is a treasure worth more than gold or precious stones. Money can buy many things, good and evil. All the wealth of the world could not buy you a friend or pay you for the loss of one.

—*C. D. Prentice*

THE HERITAGE BOOK

Our deeds are seeds of fate, sown here on earth, but bringing forth their harvest in eternity.

—G. Boardman

Trust in the Lord with all your heart. And do not lean on your own understanding. In all your ways acknowledge Him. And He will make your paths straight.

—Proverbs 3:5-6

Have courage for the great sorrows of life and patience for the small ones; and when you have laboriously accomplished your daily task, go to sleep in peace. God is awake.

—Victor Hugo

THE HERITAGE BOOK

Cream of Carrot Cheddar Soup

1	tbsp vegetable oil
1	onion, chopped
6	carrots, chopped
5	cups chicken stock (or chicken broth)
2	tbsps rice
1	tsp Worcestershire sauce
1/4	tsp dried thyme
1	tbsp parsley flakes
1	bay leaf

dash of hot pepper sauce
pinch of pepper (salt optional)

1 1/2	cups 2% milk
1	cup shredded old cheddar cheese

In a large saucepan, heat oil over medium heat; cook onion for 5 minutes (stirring occasionally). Add carrots, chicken stock, rice, Worcestershire sauce, thyme, parsley, bay leaf, hot pepper sauce, pepper; bring to a boil. Reduce heat to low and simmer 25 minutes (or until carrots are tender). Discard bay leaf. In a blender purée the soup in batches; return to pan. Stir in milk. Bring to simmer; stir in cheddar cheese and cook over low heat until melted. Add salt to taste. Makes 4 servings.

THE HERITAGE BOOK

This morning I enjoyed the sight of the many feathered friends who have become regular visitors to our backyard bird feeders.

Marg and I take turns stocking the feeders with wild seed, chunks of suet, and pine cones with peanut butter rolled in seed. The latter are usually made by our grandchildren during winter visits.

What many people may not realize is that once you start to feed the birds you must continue to do so until the snow has gone. These little creatures come to depend on the food and there is a good chance they will starve if their food supply is sporadic or cut off altogether.

This morning's guests included numerous brown sparrows, chickadees, two cardinals and my personal favourite, a blue jay.

It really does feel good to help some of God's smaller creatures.

Tell me who admires and loves you, and I will tell you who you are.

—*Charles Augustin Sainte-Beuve*

THE HERITAGE BOOK

A SURVEY taken among a group of children proves what many of us have felt for years: television violence has a profound effect on young people.

The survey used a group of ten-year-olds who watched about two hours of television a day.

Without exception the children agreed that there were things seen on television, or in the movies, that terrified them. One child told of seeing a movie where a murderer suddenly jumped from a closet. This particular scene so frightened him that he was afraid to go near his own closet for weeks.

Most of the children felt that horrible things stick in the mind for some time, and the more frightened they were the longer it took to rid their minds of the terror. When asked if seeing violence changed their behaviour, one little girl said that she often lost her appetite or became less talkative for a period of time.

All the children agreed that they want guidance from parents for acceptable viewing.

"Even if we argue our parents should make the decisions and stick to them." Interesting, isn't it?

SATURDAY — FEBRUARY 11

O READER! had you in your mind
Such stores as silent thought can bring,
O gentle Reader! you would find
A tale in everything.

—*William Wordsworth*

SUNDAY — FEBRUARY 12

TRULY, truly I say to you, he who hears My
word, and believes Him who sent Me, has
eternal life, and does not come into judgement
but has passed out of death into life.

—*John 5:24*

MONDAY — FEBRUARY 13

OH, write of me, not "Died in bitter pains,"
But "Emigrated to another star!"

—*Helen Hunt Jackson*

TUESDAY — FEBRUARY 14

Valentine's Day

THY love is such I can in no way repay,
The heavens reward thee manifold, I pray.
Then while we live, in love let's so persevere
That when we live no more, we may live ever.
—*Anne Bradstreet*

WEDNESDAY — FEBRUARY 15

As a senior on a fixed income I have found the cost of entertaining friends at dinner to be prohibitive. What was once a weekly ritual has become an infrequent luxury.

My friend Lillian has suggested a nice alternative.

"Four of us who enjoy getting together regularly 'pool' our refrigerator items each Saturday evening. Extra carrots, bits of cheese, pasta, and small amounts of ground beef can be combined to make a wonderful casserole. Much of the fun comes from concocting our unusual menu. We are able to dine together regularly for a very reasonable cost."

Since Eve ate apples, much depends on dinner.

—*Lord Byron*

THE HERITAGE BOOK

THURSDAY — FEBRUARY 16

No man is an island entire of itself: every man is a piece of the continent, a part of the main. If a clod be washed away by the sea, Europe is the less, as well as if a promontory were, as well as if a manor of thy friend's or of thine own were. Any man's death diminishes me, because I am involved in mankind. Therefore never send to know for whom the bell tolls. It tolls for thee.

—*John Donne*

FRIDAY — FEBRUARY 17

Avoiding danger is no safer in the long run than outright exposure. The fearful are caught as often as the bold.

—*Helen Keller*

SATURDAY — FEBRUARY 18

I'll not listen to reason. Reason always means what someone else has got to say.

—*Elizabeth Cleghorn Gaskell*

THE HERITAGE BOOK

An excellent wife, who can find? For her worth is far above jewels.

—Proverbs 31:10

Monday — February 20

Many retired Canadians have renewed their interest in learning. Rather than signing up for traditional instructor-led classes, however, they are choosing to direct their own courses of study.

Several universities are now offering non-credit "peer learning" programs in which study groups of usually three to fifteen people select a topic, research it for themselves, and then present it for discussion.

For around fifty dollars per group member the universities provide study space, access to research facilities, and resource people to guide the development of learning skills.

Several of the universities also help individuals locate others wishing to join a group.

If you live near a university and are interested it is well worth looking into.

THE HERITAGE BOOK

My friends and I agree that the great joy of being a grandparent or great-grandparent is that you are free to enjoy the children without the responsibility involved in their rearing. I offer you today some other ideas on grandparents and grandparenting.

No one who has not known that inestimable privilege can possibly realize what good fortune it is to grow up in a home where there are grandparents.

—*Suzanne LaFollette*

Grandma always made you feel she had been waiting to see just you all day and now the day was complete.

—*Marcy Demaree*

If your baby is "beautiful and perfect, never cries or fusses, sleeps on schedule and burps on demand, an angel all the time" . . . you're the grandma.

—*Teresa Bloomingdale*

THE HERITAGE BOOK

On this day in 1992 my sister Sarah and her husband Richard were married. For them it has been a "marriage made in heaven."

Richard, a widower, has found in Sarah a love and companionship that he felt he would never have again after the death of his first wife.

This is Sarah's first marriage, but as she says now, "Perhaps waiting so long to find Richard has just made me appreciate him all the more."

Grow old along with me!
The best is yet to be,
The last of life for which the first was made.
                                    —Robert Browning

Driving as if you were on your way to the dentist's is a good safe speed.
                                    —G. Sands

THE HERITAGE BOOK

Babies are nature's way of showing people what the world looks like at two a.m.

My daughter Julia gave me a very special gift today. Knowing how fond I am of the work of Trisha Romance, the well-known young Canadian artist, she presented me with a signed, framed print entitled "The Museum Trip."

"I just happened to be at a showing of Trisha's work and I remembered how much you liked her art."

This artist's work depicts scenes from the turn of the century. Her attention to detail is most impressive, from the decorative gingerbread trim on the homes to the candled chandeliers in the bedrooms. Her work gives the feeling that the scenes could be old photographs to which colour has been added.

As my former readers know this is the very style to which my taste in artwork runs. What a delightful gift!

THE HERITAGE BOOK

THIS morning at church we sang one of my favourite hymns. I hope it is one of your favourites as well.

Holy, Holy, Holy! Lord God Almighty!
Early in the morning our song shall rise to
    Thee!
Holy, Holy, Holy! Merciful and mighty.
God in Three Persons, Blessed Trinity!

IMAGINATION! who can sing thy force?
Or who describe the swiftness of thy course?
Soaring through air to find the bright abode,
Th'empyreal palace of the thund'ring God,
We on thy pinions can surpass the wind,
And leave the rolling universe behind:
From star to star the mental optics rove,
Measure the skies, and range the realms
    above.
There in one view we grasp the mighty whole,
Or with new worlds amaze th'unbounded soul.
—Phillis Wheatley

THE HERITAGE BOOK

A T White Otter Lake, forty-eight kilometres south of Ignace in northern Ontario, a deserted three-storey log castle rests in the midst of the wilderness. The castle was completed just before 1914 by Jimmy McQuat, a Scot who arrived here in 1903 and earned a living from trapping and fishing.

McQuat's motive for building the castle has remained a puzzle. According to one story it was built for a sweetheart, a noble Scottish lady, but this was never proved.

Whatever the motive, this small man in his fifties felled logs, hauled them through the bush, squared the sides, dovetailed the ends, and then raised the walls and roof. The heavy imported windows were carried by canoe over fifteen portages.

Sadly, McQuat never obtained the title to the land on which the castle stood. To the government he was just a squatter.

In October 1918 Jimmy McQuat became tangled in his own fish nets and drowned. He was buried near his log castle.

In the 1980's Ignace adopted the castle as a civic symbol. Today adventurous travellers can reach the castle by logging road and snowshoes (or canoes in summer).

March

Ash Wednesday

ALMIGHTY and everlasting God, who hatest nothing that thou hast made and dost forgive the sins of all them that are penitent: Create and make in us new and contrite hearts, that we worthily lamenting our sins, and acknowledging our wretchedness, may obtain of thee, the God of all mercy, perfect remission and forgiveness; through Jesus Christ our Lord. Amen.

With this prayer we begin the Lenten season, a most important time for those of us who embrace the Christian faith. I hope you will enjoy a renewal of your faith, whatever it may be.

THE HERITAGE BOOK

After Boccaccio wrote to the elderly Italian poet Petrarch urging him to give up writing and take life easy he received this reply.

"I am conscious of the love that prompts you to give me medical advice although you don't heed it in your own case. Please pardon me if I don't obey you. Constant, persistent labour is the food of my mind. When I begin to slow down and take repose I shall soon cease to live.

"Reading and writing, which you tell me to reduce, are only a slight task or rather they are a pleasant relaxation that makes one forget serious labour. Nothing weighs less than a pen, nothing is more cheering. Other pleasures flee and leave depressions behind, but a pen allures you when you take it up and delights you when you lay it down. I think that one may properly say that of all earthly delights, none is more noble than literature, none longer-lasting, sweeter, more constant, none that so readily endows its practitioner with a splendid cloak for every circumstance without cost or trouble.

"So forgive me, my dear brother, forgive me: I shall believe you in all else, but not in this advice of yours."

FRIDAY — MARCH 3

HERE are two things that you'd like to hear from your dentist—but probably won't:

"I think you're flossing too much."

"I won't ask you any questions until I take the pick out of your mouth."

SATURDAY — MARCH 4

THE greatest man is he who chooses the right with invincible resolution; who resists the sorest temptation from within and without; who bears the heaviest burdens cheerfully; who is calmest in storms, and most fearless under menace and frowns; and whose reliance on truth, on virtue, and on God, is most unfaltering.

—*Author unknown*

SUNDAY — MARCH 5

LET not thine hand be stretched out to receive, and shut when thou shouldest pay.
—*Ecclesiastes 4:20*

THE HERITAGE BOOK

MONDAY — MARCH 6

THE rung of a ladder was never meant to rest upon, but only to hold a man's foot long enough to enable him to put the other somewhat higher.

—Thomas Henry Huxley

TUESDAY — MARCH 7

WE have not completely fulfilled our responsibility as parents until we bequeath to our children a love of books, a thirst for knowledge, a hunger for righteousness, an awareness of beauty, a memory of kindness, an understanding of loyalty, a vision of greatness, and a good name.

—William Arthur Ward

WEDNESDAY — MARCH 8

WHEREVER you are it's your own friends who make your world.

—William James

THE HERITAGE BOOK

ALTHOUGH winter is a difficult time of year for most it can be especially harsh for nursing home residents and shut-ins. Visits from friends, family and others often provide a ray of sunshine on those gloomy days when they can't get out easily.

Marg and I have been paying regular visits to our local nursing home over the past few months and we have made many new friends.

The director of nursing offered us a few tips that have proved invaluable.

• If you don't know a nursing home resident personally, visit the facility, introduce yourself to the person in charge, and say that you are interested in becoming a visitor.

• Call ahead to make sure that your visit is convenient.

• Think of things that may be interesting to talk about. Family, friends, community life long ago, and travel are but a few possibilities.

• Offers to do something helpful, such as writing a letter, making a phone call, or running an errand are much appreciated.

• Taking a conversation piece, a photo, or a magazine article is also a good way to break the ice.

THE HERITAGE BOOK

FRIDAY — MARCH 10

OUR neighbour Don gave us a good laugh this evening with this story.

For her birthday Don had given his elderly mother a cordless portable phone. Soon afterwards Don began to get an unusual number of long distance "casual" calls from his normally frugal parent. When Don asked about the frequency of her calls she replied, "Well, my goodness, why not take advantage? It can't cost a single penny—the phone isn't attached to anything!"

SATURDAY — MARCH 11

SMELL is a potent wizard that transports us across a thousand miles and all our years. The odours of fruits waft me to my southern home, to frolics in the peach orchard. Other odours, instantaneous and fleeting, cause my heart to dilate joyously or contract with remembered grief. Even as I think of smells, my nose is full of scents that awake sweet memories of summers gone and ripening grain fields far away.

—Helen Keller

THE HERITAGE BOOK

IN peace I will both lie down and sleep, for
Thou alone, O Lord, dost make me to dwell
in safety.

—Psalm 4:8

OUTDOORS, a March blizzard is raging,
Snowflakes are whirling in flight.
Whining gale at the windowpane
Echoes across the stormy night.
The spattering snow on the rooftops
Forms a downy coverlet of white,
Sweeping clouds obscure twinkling stars
Like a veil in the dim moonlight.

Indoors filled with flickering shadows,
The crackling hearthfire gleams
Gives comfort to chase away darkness;
The hissing coal-lamp casts beams.
While the chill of long winter still lingers
Lies white on the windowsill,
It ignites the grey ashes of longing,
The spark of desire burns still.

—Margaret Jewell

THE HERITAGE BOOK

Two years ago this week the eastern United States and parts of Canada were hit by the most vicious storm of the century. Stories of "The Blizzard of '93" are many and varied but I enjoyed hearing from my brother Ben and his wife Marie about their adventure.

The pair had been enjoying a scenic and leisurely drive en route to a long-planned holiday in New Orleans. As they drove through Tennessee the light rain turned quickly to snow. The wind picked up, the snow became heavier, and the driving was suddenly very difficult and hazardous.

Pulling to the side of the road to study the map Ben was surprised to see another car pull in behind him and the driver get out and approach the car.

"Hi, folks! I'm just on my way home—this storm is going to be a real dilly according to the reports. There's nothing along here for miles so you folks just follow me. My wife'll be glad for the company and you can wait out the storm in comfort."

Apparently there are angels on earth.

THE HERITAGE BOOK

CHILDREN keep on the straight and narrow best if they get good road directions from people who have travelled the route.

—*Wood Lanier*

WHEN Bruce exclaimed "My, this is an interesting article," he gave no clue to Marg and I that he was about to ruin our appetites for tonight's dinner.

"Did you know that locust dumplings are a much sought-after specialty in many Arab countries? And for heaven's sake, snake is a staple in the African country of Cameroon. The people eat snake like we eat hamburgers, Mother—it's a cheap, filling, easy-to-get meal."

Paying no heed to our lack of enthusiasm he continued, "Why it says here that mice in cream sauce is an Arctic delicacy. They marinate them in alcohol, roll them in flour, then soak them in cream sauce for ten minutes before serving."

Marg and I both left the room as Bruce went on, "Now stir-fried dog is popular in . . . ."

THE HERITAGE BOOK

Land of the sparkling Emerald Isle
And lakes of crystal sheen,
Home of the fabled leprechaun
And the luck of the shamrock green.

Forest glades where the fairies dance
With their shiny gossamer wings,
Where a violin plays an Irish air
And Patrick O'Leary sings.

The little shoemaker busy at work
Gives out his tap-tapping sound
Pride of the Irish—the red-haired colleens
And Mike's shelelah pounds.

Where at the end of the rainbow
Like the age-old story has told,
Many have searched but few have found
The coveted pot of gold.

—Margaret Jewell

Happy St. Patrick's Day to all of you who claim
Irish ancestry.

THE HERITAGE BOOK

WHAT is so important and so often over-looked in any difference of opinion is that it's not who is right but what is right.

COME to me, all you who labour and are heavy laden, and I will give you rest.

—Matthew 11:28

THERE are two things to aim at in life: first, to get what you want; and after that, to enjoy it. Only the wisest of mankind achieve the second.

—Logan Pearsall Smith

THREE years ago today our family welcomed spring in a very special way. My great-granddaughter Bethany was born, and her birthday is an ongoing reminder of this time of renewal.

THE HERITAGE BOOK

A FEW of my older friends and I were discussing our changing world. We seniors have seen incredible changes during our lifetimes and most of these changes have been very positive.

Scientific and medical advances have been mind-boggling. Men have walked on the moon; tuberculosis and polio have been virtually eliminated.

What I find difficult to cope with (and my friends agreed) is the pace of life today.

People are always in a hurry. At the grocery store I saw a can of frosting that could be put on cakes before they cooled. Has life become so fast-paced that we don't have time for cakes to cool any more?

People hurry home from work so that they can get to bed so that they can get up for work so that they can get home again. Often weekends are spent getting a head start on next week. Cooking, cleaning, laundry all need doing so that one is not "behind."

A sense of hurry is the norm now but it is not natural. I feel that life would be enjoyed so much more if it weren't being enjoyed so quickly.

Thursday — March 23

We celebrate every birthday, we celebrate Easter, Christmas, New Year's Day, and every other day we can think of. To me ritual is the glue that keeps society together. Family rituals, like vacations with the whole family, are very important things. To give a sense of community; that is what gives people peace of mind and security.

—*Pierre Berton*

Friday — March 24

Don't spend your precious time asking "Why isn't all the world a better place?" It will only be time wasted. The question to ask is "How can I make it better?" To that question, there is an answer.

—*Leo F. Buscaglia*

Saturday — March 25

Without libraries what have we? We have no past and no future.

—*Ray Bradbury*

THE HERITAGE BOOK

GRANT, we beseech thee, Almighty God, that we, who for our evil deeds do worthily deserve to be punished, by the comfort of thy grace may mercifully be relieved; through our Lord and Saviour, Jesus Christ.
> —*Collect for the fourth Sunday in Lent*

MONDAY — MARCH 27

A KEEN sense of humour helps us to overlook the unbecoming, understand the unconventional, tolerate the unpleasant, overcome the unexpected, and outlast the unbearable.
> —*Billy Graham*

TUESDAY — MARCH 28

SAYS actor Tom Selleck, "Whenever I get full of myself, I remember the nice elderly couple who approached me with a camera on a street in Honolulu one day. When I struck a pose for them, the man said, 'No, no, we want you to take a picture of us.'"

THE HERITAGE BOOK

My son-in-law John, a minister, amused us with this story this evening.

A group of ecumenical doctoral students was discussing sermon preparation. A Baptist minister explained that he devoted the month of July to writing a year's worth of sermons. His Presbyterian colleague said that he outlined on Mondays and wrote his final drafts on the following days.

The rabbi used Wednesday mornings for preparation and the Catholic priest admitted that he often used Saturday evenings to meet the Sunday deadline.

The Anglican priest gave everyone a good laugh as he said "Well . . . I usually schedule a long hymn before the sermon."

I like living. I have sometimes been wildly, despairingly, acutely miserable, racked with sorrow, but through it all I still know quite certainly that just to be alive is a grand thing.
—*Agatha Christie*

THE HERITAGE BOOK

SEVERAL of the poems in this year's book were
written by an old friend, Margaret Jewell.

Margaret is a native of the Rainy River
district in northern Ontario. She was born in
the village of Emo and most of her early years
were spent there. Her school years were
spread between Emo, Lash, and Dance, all in
the Rainy River area.

For most of her married life Margaret and
her husband Lloyd resided on a farm in
Aylsworth.

When she was a young schoolgirl Margaret
discovered that she enjoyed writing poetry. As
she married and raised a family she kept up
her writing, using her vivid imagination and
excellent memory to record her life and times
in this remote area of the province.

It is the "homey" and unpretentious quality
of her work that I find appealing.

I hope that you will enjoy her offerings as
well.

April

ON this "April Fools Day" I thought of a number of people who fooled many by their successes.

Big-time winning jockey Eddie Arcaro rode in 250 races before he ever won.

Basketball great Michael Jordan was cut from his high school basketball team as a sophomore by a coach who told him he just wasn't good enough.

John Grisham, best-selling author of *The Firm, The Client,* and *The Pelican Brief* had his first novel rejected by twenty-eight publishers.

THE HERITAGE BOOK

SUNDAY — APRIL 2

W^E beseech thee, Almighty God, mercifully to look upon thy people; that by thy great goodness they may be governed and preserved evermore, both in body and soul; through Jesus Christ our Lord.

—Collect for the fifth Sunday in Lent

MONDAY — APRIL 3

S^{PRING} is a lively season in northwest Prince Edward Island, especially for the farming communities in Prince County, where half the province's potato crop is grown.

The common white, or Irish potato—introduced by settlers in the late 1700's—thrives in P.E.I.'s temperate climate and red sandy soil. Spring sees nearly 10,000 hectares planted with thirty-two varieties of "spuds."

Roughly fifty percent of the annual crop is sold for the table. Another fifteen percent is processed there and the remainder is sold as seed stock. P.E.I. seed potatoes have been used to start crops in eighteen countries.

As we enjoy our potatoes at dinner let us give thanks to the hard-working farmers of our smallest province.

THE HERITAGE BOOK

Hospitalization can be a frightening experience for children, especially when parents are unable to be with them.

Several years ago the Children's Hospital in Orange County, California, came up with a new way to reassure young patients. They videotaped mothers reading stories, then showed them to the children when Mom was away.

As well as their child's favourite story, the mothers read *The Missing Piece Meets the Big O* by Shel Silverstein and *The Runaway Bunny* by Margaret Wise Brown. Both describe separations and reunions, and seem to have much success in alleviating children's fears of separation.

O! how this spring of love resembleth
The uncertain glory of an April day!
—*William Shakespeare*

THE HERITAGE BOOK

As the hockey season ends and we head into the playoffs I think back to 1993 and memories of the remarkable season enjoyed by the Toronto Maple Leaf team.

Our family has long been Leaf fans but even the most die-hard of us couldn't have imagined that this group of players could make it to the semi-finals of the Stanley Cup Championships.

The first big surprise came when the fourth-place-finishing Leafs eliminated the first-place Chicago Black Hawks, who were believed to be bigger, better, faster, and stronger than Toronto.

The Leafs then moved on to face the St. Louis Blues. Felix (the "Cat") Potvin and Doug Gilmour put on incredible displays of goal-tending and goal scoring to lead the Leafs to the division championship and a berth in the semi-finals against the Los Angeles Kings.

Although Los Angeles eventually eliminated the Leafs it was a titanic struggle. Several games went into overtime and each player gave it everything he had.

Players and fans had a right to be proud of an exciting season. As for this year? "Go Leafs, Go!"

THE HERITAGE BOOK

Friday — April 7

A LITTLE kingdom I possess,
Where thoughts and feelings dwell;
And very hard the task I find
Of governing it well.

—Louisa May Alcott

Saturday — April 8

L IFE is to be lived to its fullest so that death is just another chapter. Memories of our lives, our works and our deeds will continue in others.

—Rosa Parks

Sunday — April 9

P ILATE said to them, "Then what shall I do with Jesus who is called Christ?" They all said "Let him be crucified!"

—Matthew 27:22

THE HERITAGE BOOK

WE cannot tell the precise moment when friendship is formed. As in filling a vessel drop by drop, there is at last a drop which makes it run over; so in a series of kindnesses there is at last one which makes the heart run over.

—James Boswell

ONE problem with growing old is that we face the loss of dear friends on a frighteningly regular basis. Trips to the funeral home remind us of our own vulnerability and make us all too aware of the speedy passing of time.

My great faith in life in the hereafter allows me to accept death as simply another step in a natural progression. James Montgomery's lines express my thoughts very well.

If God made this world so fair
Where sin and death abound,
How beautiful beyond compare
Will paradise be found.

THE HERITAGE BOOK

My dear friend Betty never ceases to amaze me. An invalid for years and confined to her home, she is never idle.

"I have a new hobby, Edna," she informed me during my visit today. "I have taken up découpage and I am enjoying it immensely."

Découpage is the art of decorating surfaces with paper cutouts. It first became popular during the eighteenth century when Italian apprentices applied coloured engravings to furniture in order to imitate expensive hand-painted pieces. Called "the poor man's art" it produced very beautiful furniture, some of which can be seen in museums today.

As Betty explained, "Though it's quite simple, taste, patience, planning, and careful workmanship are important if your work is to be well done."

Betty started with small wooden boxes purchased from a crafts store which she decorated with cutouts from art books. Since then she has decorated trays and glass plates, and is now working on a lamp base.

Betty's generous nature showed itself again as she donated several pieces to be sold at the church's Spring Fair.

THE HERITAGE BOOK

WHAT is so rare as a first sign of spring
When you look at willow tree, budding
 with green,
And out of that bud peers a downy wee fellow,
So soft and so plushy, oval and mellow.

The gentle spring rain, and rays of warm sun
Portray what a miracle nature has done,
When out of its vest, pops a little grey pillow,
In all of its wonder—the first pussy willow!
—*Margaret Jewell*

Good Friday

AND Jesus crying out with a loud voice said
"Father, Into Thy Hands I Commit My
Spirit." And having said this, He breathed
His last.
—*Luke 23:46*

SATURDAY — APRIL 15

O N his 70th birthday Henry Wadsworth Longfellow wrote this letter to a friend.

"You do not know yet what it is to be seventy years old. I will tell you, so that you may not be taken by surprise when your turn comes. It is like climbing the Alps. You reach a snow-crowned summit, and see behind you the deep valley stretching miles and miles away, and before you other summits higher and whiter which you may have strength to climb, or may not. Then you sit down and meditate and wonder which it will be. This is the whole story, amplify it as you may. All that one can say is that life is opportunity."

SUNDAY — APRIL 16

Easter Sunday

A ND He said to them "Thus it is written, that the Christ should suffer and rise again from the dead on the third day; and that repentance for forgiveness of sins should be proclaimed in His name to all nations beginning from Jerusalem."

—*Luke 24:46-47*

THE HERITAGE BOOK

My friend Mary McConnell and her husband Bob are raising ten children, an astonishing number when you consider today's economy.

"Vacations have always been a huge expense for us so this year we are going to try something different. We are trading homes with a family from St. John, New Brunswick.

"Jim works in the St. John office of Bob's company. He had mentioned that he would like to bring his family to see our area of southern Ontario, so Bob suggested the exchange of homes for the first two weeks of July.

"Jim was enthusiastic, and so we'll be spending our holiday visiting such interesting places as Reversing Falls, the New Brunswick Museum, Old City Market, Saint John Shipbuilding and Dry Dock, and the many other points of interest in this old city. Jim and his family are planning to visit Ontario Place, the CN Tower, SkyDome, and the Science Centre. Without the exorbitant costs of motels and restaurants we'll be able to enjoy a longer holiday with extra money for sightseeing."

This seems to be an ideal way for us seniors to holiday as well.

TUESDAY — APRIL 18

My dear friend and neighbour Lila and I enjoyed a lovely spring walk today. Lila is using a walker now so we don't travel as far afield as we once did. Nonetheless it was wonderful to get out and smell the clean fresh air and to see the progress of the flowers as they poke through the thawed ground.

On today's outing we saw lots of crocuses in full bloom but the daffodils, tulips and hyacinths are just shoots coming up. Of all the early flowers the hyacinths are my favourites. Their perfume is unrivalled, and cross breeding has produced some beautiful pink, mauve, and deep purple hues.

There really is no better way to enjoy a spring day than by seeing God's wonders in the company of a good friend.

WEDNESDAY — APRIL 19

There's a time when you have to explain to your children why they're born, and it's a marvellous thing if you know the reason by then.

—Hazel Scott

THE HERITAGE BOOK

Thursday — April 20

In 1894 a young girl from Newmarket, Ontario made up a story about a girl named Nancy who was so poor that she ate potato peelings. She sent her story to "The Youth's Companion," which was running a contest for authors under age sixteen.

Her story didn't win but a note was attached to the returned manuscript. It read: "You are very young to have entered the competition, but if the promise shown by this story is fulfilled you will make a good writer one day."

Mazo de la Roche was only nine at the time.

Friday — April 21

Call the world if you please "The vale of soul-making."

—John Keats

Saturday — April 22

Down in their hearts, wise people know this truth: the only way to help yourself is to help others.

THE HERITAGE BOOK

MANY are the sorrows of the wicked; But he who trusts in the Lord, loving kindness shall surround him. Be glad in the Lord and rejoice you righteous ones, and shout for joy all you who are upright in heart.

—Psalm 32:10-11

OUR Lord has written the promise of the Resurrection, not in books alone, but in every leaf in Springtime.

—Martin Luther

THERE is no friend like an old friend
Who has shared our morning days.
No greeting like his welcome,
No homage like his praise.

—Oliver Wendell Holmes

THE HERITAGE BOOK

Just about five years ago now my friend Peggy, who lives in the Cotswald Hills in England, began a bold venture. Her husband John had passed away and she was living on a small pension in a pretty home. She redecorated her two upstairs bedrooms, added a modern bathroom, and turned her house into a "Bed and Breakfast" tourist home. It has been a "smashing" success.

In her last letter Peggy's enthusiasm knew no bounds.

"I can't begin to tell you how much I enjoy this, Edna. I have had visitors from all over the world in my home. Many of my guests are seniors who enjoy an affordable place to stay in a beautiful area of our country. One couple from Des Moines, Iowa, stayed with me for a whole month while they made day trips around the countryside. Often I will accompany my guests to the pub for dinner so that they can meet the local folk and get a real feel for life in our village. As well, the extra bit of money coming in has made my life more comfortable."

It's so nice to hear of someone whose business venture has turned out well and gives them so much pleasure.

Thursday — April 27

My grandson Fred was persuaded by his family to visit a neighbouring farm where there was a litter of new Labrador pups.

On the way there Fred repeated over and over, "We have two pets already. We're just going to *look!*"

They arrived at the farm and went to the barn to see the dogs. Fred looked at the one yellow pup in the black litter and said, "We'll take that one."

June and the boys haven't stopped laughing yet.

Friday — April 28

It is easy to fool yourself. It is possible to fool the people you work for. It is more difficult to fool the people you work with. But it is impossible to fool the people who work under you.

—*Harry B. Thayer*

Saturday — April 29

THE art of medicine consists of keeping the patient in a good mood while nature does the healing.

—Voltaire

Sunday — April 30

THIS morning's church service was a very happy occasion. Five infants were received into Christ's holy church through the service of baptism. It is encouraging to see many young couples returning to the church and bringing up their children to be a part of the large Christian family.

And they were bringing children to Him so that He might touch them; and the disciples rebuked them. But when Jesus saw this He was indignant and said to them "Permit the children to come to Me; do not hinder them; for the kingdom of God belongs to such as these. Truly I say unto you, whoever does not receive the kingdom of God like a child shall not enter it at all."

—Mark 10:13-15

May

A ·DELICATE fabric of bird song
Floats in the air
The smell of wet wild earth
Is everywhere.

Red small leaves of the maple
Are clenched like a hand
Like girls at their first communion
The pear trees stand.

Oh I must pass nothing by
Without loving it much,
The raindrop try with my lips,
The grass with my touch;

For how can I be sure
I shall see again
The world on the first of May
Shining after the rain?

—*Sara Teasdale*

THE HERITAGE BOOK

My friend Will, an avid gardener, recently purchased several new tools, and he is looking forward to using them in his gardens.

"The hardware store owner must have a good sense of humour, Edna. He enclosed a paper with some 'Definitions for Home Gardeners.' I enjoyed a good laugh and I thought your readers might also."

Annual: Any plant that dies before blooming.

Brochures and Catalogues: Forms of entertaining fiction that are published by nurseries, seed companies, and tool manufacturers.

Furrow: Horizontal line on the forehead of a gardener.

Hoe: Gardening tool whose name derives from the fact that when its blade is stepped on, its handle delivers a sharp rap to the gardener's brow at which point he or she cries "Ho!"

Perennial: Any plant which, had it lived, would have bloomed year after year.

Rot: Gardening advice.

WEDNESDAY — MAY 3

IT is in our memories that we find ourselves, and the parts of ourselves that make us what we are today. And it is in our love of the past that we find our commitment to the present— and our hope for the future.

—Merle Shain

THURSDAY — MAY 4

IF you have made mistakes there is always another chance for you; you may have a fresh start any moment you choose, for this thing we call "failure" is not the falling down, but the staying down.

—Mary Pickford

FRIDAY — MAY 5

THE object of true education is to make people not merely to do the right things, but enjoy them; not merely industrious, but to love industry; not merely learned but to love knowledge; not merely pure, but to love purity; not merely just, but to hunger and thirst after justice.

—John Ruskin

THE HERITAGE BOOK

An old friend travelling through Golden, British Columbia included this interesting story in her letter today.

"Once there was a St. Peter's Anglican Church, 30 km north of Golden, at Donald. Today this church is in Windermere, 125 km south, minus its original bell and known as St. Peter's the Stolen. The bell is in Golden, in St. Paul's of the Stolen Bell.

"The theft of the church (and bell) happened back in 1897. When the Canadian Pacific Railway abandoned Donald in favour of Revelstoke the bishop decided that St. Peter's should go there too. However, zealous St. Peter's people moving to Windermere dismantled their church and took it with them by rail and barge. En route, in Golden, the bell was pilfered by the equally enterprising Anglicans of Golden, and thus the name of Golden's Anglican Church, St. Paul's of the Stolen Bell."

This is the day which the Lord has made; Let us rejoice and be glad in it.

—Psalm 118:24

THE HERITAGE BOOK

Monday — May 8

I AM a great believer in luck, and I find the harder I work the more I have of it.

—*Thomas Jefferson*

Tuesday — May 9

I READ a most interesting article today in *The Journal of the American Medical Association*. It claimed that people who live alone after a heart attack are almost twice as likely as those with household companions to suffer a second attack or die within six months. One reason loners are at a higher risk is that help is not at hand if an emergency arises. But researchers also think that living with others benefits overall health.

When I think of my own circle of friends I have no trouble believing the experts. Those of my friends who live with loved ones or other care-givers seem to be enjoying better health than those who are living alone.

Of course there are always exceptions in every situation but I certainly feel that the good health I enjoy is due in large part to the fact that I am living with my family.

THE HERITAGE BOOK

BLESSED are they who have the gift of making friends, for it is one of God's best gifts. It involves many things, but above all, the power of going out of one's self, and appreciating whatever is noble and loving in another.

—Thomas Hughes

SOME people find it very difficult to say no. With today's hectic pace and the many demands placed on people's time and energies it is important to be able to say no in a pleasant but firm way.

Actor Paul Newman was dining with a friend at a restaurant when he was approached by a man asking for his autograph. "Sorry, but that's not something I do," was the actor's polite but firm reply.

Some other pleasant but appropriate responses I have heard are "That's an excellent offer but we're not in a position to take advantage of it right now," or "About Saturday, it just won't work for me." To refuse an invitation, I like "I always enjoy myself when I'm with you so I'm really sorry that I can't make it."

THE HERITAGE BOOK

FRIDAY — MAY 12

To live is so startling it leaves little time for anything else.

—*Emily Dickinson*

SATURDAY — MAY 13

If you are patient in one moment of anger, you will escape a hundred days of sorrow.

—*Chinese epigram*

SUNDAY — MAY 14

Mother's Day

Father in Heaven, make me wise,
So that my gaze may never meet
A question in my children's eyes;
God keep me always kind and sweet …

A mother's day is very long,
There are so many things to do!
But never let me lose my song
Before the hardest day is through.

—*Margaret Sangster*

THE HERITAGE BOOK

MONDAY — MAY 15

HOPE is wishing for a thing to come true; faith is believing that it will come true.

—Norman Vincent Peale

TUESDAY — MAY 16

MY friend Jake Frampton gave me a book written by television personality David Frost and a business associate Micheal Deakin. The book is entitled *David Frost's Book of the World's Worst Decisions.*

Frost's favourite was the story of Sam Phillips of Memphis, Tennessee, who in 1955 sold to R.C.A. Victor Records his exclusive contract with a young singer named Elvis Presley. As it turned out Phillips forfeited royalties on more than a billion records.

WEDNESDAY — MAY 17

THE trouble is, if you don't risk anything, you risk even more.

—Erica Jong

THE HERITAGE BOOK

WHOEVER first said that "dog is man's best friend" was really on to something. "Project Safe Run" was founded in 1981 by Shelley Reecher of Eugene, Oregon. This fast-growing organization trains dogs to defend runners, senior citizens, women who work late shifts, and others who don't feel safe out alone.

Shelley, herself a rape survivor, trained a Doberman to run with her while she was attending the University of Oregon. So many of her classmates borrowed Jake when they went running that Shelley adopted and trained six more dogs within six months.

She bought a house to keep her canine friends and continued to train more animals.

For a fee of twenty-five dollars a month (free for seniors) runners and others have unlimited access to Safe Run's trained dogs.

Feeling safe when you are out alone is very important, and the dogs offer that sense of security.

READING is to the mind what exercise is to the body.

THE HERITAGE BOOK

SATURDAY — MAY 20

THERE is no beautifier of complexion, or form, or behaviour, like the wish to scatter joy and not pain around us.

—Ralph Waldo Emerson

SUNDAY — MAY 21

LORD in Thy name thy servants plead,
And Thou hast sworn to hear;
Thine is the harvest, Thine the seed,
The fresh and fading year.

Our hope when autumn winds blew wild
The trusted Lord, with Thee;
And still now spring has on us smiled,
We wait on thy decree.

The former and the latter rain,
The summer sun and air
The green air, and the golden grain,
All Thine are ours by prayer.

—John Keble

THE HERITAGE BOOK

HERE in the Muskoka cottage country Marg, Bruce and I enjoyed the traditional "cottage opening" weekend with our good friend Eleanor.

Many years ago, after Eleanor's husband passed away, she was concerned about coming to the cottage alone.

"Bob did all the larger physical jobs; he turned on the power and the water and made sure that all the pipes were clear and uncracked. He gave the deck chairs a fresh coat of paint, and put the boat in the water after adjusting the engine."

The thought of coming north and facing this alone was overwhelming. Then Bruce told her he would be happy to lend his handyman skills, and the rest, as they say, is history. Marg, Eleanor and I change the bedding, dust, vacuum, and see to the multitude of small but important jobs that ensure a happy, work-free summer.

After our labours on Saturday we took a short drive to the local marina, where a magnificent display of fireworks lit up the evening sky.

We were a tired but happy crew who went to bed that night.

THE HERITAGE BOOK

TUESDAY — MAY 23

WE flatter those we scarcely know,
We please the fleeting guest,
And deal full many a thoughtless blow
To those who love us best.
—*Ella Wheeler Wilcox*

WEDNESDAY — MAY 24

THIS is the birthdate of Queen Victoria of England. Born in 1819, she came to the throne as a young woman and ruled Britain until her death in 1901. There are probably many historians who remember the birth of this beloved monarch as one of the great dates in history.

THURSDAY — MAY 25

Ascension Day

HE was lifted up while they were looking on, and a cloud received Him out of their sight.

—*Acts 1:9*

THE HERITAGE BOOK

Labour to keep alive in your breast that little spark of celestial fire—conscience.
—*George Washington*

It is my joy in life to find
At every turning of the road
The strong arm of a comrade kind
To help me onward with my load.
And since I have no gold to give
And love alone must make amends,
My only prayer is, while I live—
God make me worthy of my friends.
—*Frank Dempster Sherman*

I am the light of the world; he that follows Me will not walk in darkness but shall have the light of life.

—*John 8:12*

THE HERITAGE BOOK

Yesterday was "D-Day" at our house (the D standing for diet) and I have a feeling that it could be a long few weeks coming up.

Marg and Bruce noticed that they had both amassed a few extra pounds over the winter. As they tried on their summer clothes they both realized that their shorts and light-weight pants had become uncomfortably tight after the long winter.

"Good heavens, Mother," Bruce moaned, "one good deep breath and the buttons will fly like orbiting space capsules."

And so, as of yesterday, Marg and Bruce are on a strict regimen of high fibre and low fat and, as Bruce has complained, "No good stuff!"

For someone who enjoys food as much as Bruce this is a form of torture. However, both he and Marg are determined to lose the unwanted weight and I wish them good luck and good healthy eating.

Live each day as if it were your last because one of these days you'll be right.

THE HERITAGE BOOK

My sister related a very funny story in her letter today and I hope you are amused by it as well.

Sarah was anxious to get to the market early one morning, so instead of taking the time to clean the house before heading off she simply left things as they were and figured on doing the tidying up when she got back.

Her door was left unlocked as usual and when she came home several hours later she was astonished by the sight that greeted her.

The dishes were done and the floor shone, as did the stove and refrigerator.

The bed was made, clothes had been hung up, and the living room and dining room had been dusted and vacuumed.

"I couldn't understand it at all—until later that evening when my neighbour Jean called and the mystery was solved. Apparently Jean had hired a cleaning lady from a local company and the cleaner had failed to arrive, much to Jean's dismay. It seems that the company had mixed up the house numbers."

I hope Jean was able to laugh about it.

June

Today's poem of love is a tribute to my late husband George, on our anniversary.

Because you love me, I have found
New joys that were not mine before;
New stars have lightened up my sky
With glories growing more and more.

Because you love me I can choose
To look through your dear eyes and see
Beyond the beauty of the now
Far forward to Eternity.

Because you love me I can wait
With perfect patience well possessed;
Because you love me all my life
Is circled with unquestioned rest;
Yes, even Life and Death
Is all unquestioned and all blest.

—Author unknown

THE HERITAGE BOOK

My friend Jake, an avid baseball fan, related this funny story as we enjoyed the Blue Jays game on television.

Several years ago George Steinbrenner, owner of the New York Yankees, was banned for life from the game of baseball. Short years thereafter this decision was reversed and Steinbrenner returned once again to the helm of the Yankee team.

A sportswriter for one of the New York papers wrote in his column, "George Steinbrenner was banned for life from the game of baseball. He is now back as head of the New York Yankees. Does this mean he's dead?"

The world is a looking glass, and gives back to every man the reflection of his own face. Frown at it and it will look sourly upon you; laugh at it and with it, and it is a jolly, kind companion; so let all young persons take their choice.

—*William Makepeace Thackeray*

THE HERITAGE BOOK

THEN if you confess with your mouth Jesus as Lord, and believe in your heart that God raised Him from the dead, you shall be saved.

—Romans 10:19

A VEGETABLE that I enjoy very much at this time of year is asparagus. My husband George had to be coaxed gently, spear by spear, to try it often enough to come to really love it as I did. Eventually we would even make a meal of just asparagus with a slice of bread and butter.

For the health conscious, asparagus is a good source of fibre and contains vitamin A, several B vitamins, some calcium, and ascorbic acid.

Fresh asparagus should have firm green heads and equal size stalks so that they cook evenly. When properly prepared the stalks remain bright green and firm. The microwave seems to be the best way to cook this vegetable to perfection.

Whichever way you prepare it, asparagus is an excellent way to welcome the summer.

THE HERITAGE BOOK

EIGHTY years old! No eyes left, no ears, no teeth, no legs, no wind! And when all is said and done, how astonishingly well one does without them!

—*Paul Claudel*

EVERY year of my life I grow more convinced that it is wisest and best to fix our attention on the beautiful and the good, and dwell as little as possible on the evil and false.

—*Richard Cecil*

ENDEAVOUR to be always patient of the faults and imperfections of others, for thou hast many faults and imperfections of thine own that require a reciprocation of forebearance. If thou art not able to make thyself that which thou wishest to be, how canst thou expect to mould another in conformity to thy will?

—*Thomas à Kempis*

THE HERITAGE BOOK

TODAY, my birthday, was one of the nicest that I can remember. I borrowed an idea from an old friend and I enjoyed the results immensely. It goes like this ....

When one reaches a ripe old age such as mine it is silly for friends and family to spend hard-earned money on gifts. I have everything that I could possibly want and I don't like to picture people I love wandering from store to store saying, "What in heaven's name shall we get Mother/Grandma/Edna for her birthday?"

Instead, friends and family who would be celebrating with me received a note that read: "If you would like to wish me a very happy birthday please take the money that you would usually spend on my gift and use it on yourself. Try to use it on something that would really please you. What I would like in return is a note telling me about 'my gift.'"

This evening as friends and family gathered here to celebrate my birthday I was thrilled to receive cards from everyone in attendance. We all enjoyed reading the notes to see how the others had chosen to use their "gift."

I must thank Donald Dixon for his excellent idea.

THE HERITAGE BOOK

SATURDAY — JUNE 10

ALL truly wise thoughts have been thought already thousands of times; but to make them really ours we must think them over and over again honestly, till they take firm root in our personal experience.

—*Goethe*

SUNDAY — JUNE 11

ALL things bright and beautiful
All creatures great and small,
All things wise and wonderful—
The Lord God made them all.

Each little flower that opens
Each little bird that sings—
He made their glowing colours,
He made their tiny wings.

The cold wind in the winter,
The pleasant summer sun,
The ripe fruits in the garden—
He made them every one.

—*Cecil Frances Alexander*

THE HERITAGE BOOK

SEVERAL years ago I had the great pleasure of seeing the musical "Les Misérables" at the Royal Alexandra Theatre in Toronto. The role of Jean Valjean was played by Michael Burgess, and I don't believe any singer has moved me more before or since.

Although he had been involved in many productions before "Les Miz" it was his stirring rendition of Jean Valjean that made Canadians sit up and take notice.

Recognition of his talent brought many different opportunities. In 1992 Burgess was named an honorary member of the 1992 Olympic Team in Barcelona, Spain. There he sang a tune commissioned for the CTV coverage of the games. It was magnificent!

One of his best memories is of the "All-Star" baseball game at SkyDome in Toronto. He sang the American national anthem (Alannah Myles did O Canada), and as he left the field baseball great Ted Williams said, "Son, that was outstanding! What part of the States are you from?"

Burgess' early years were a struggle to make ends meet. His hard work and outstanding talent have brought him a long way in a difficult business where few succeed.

TUESDAY — JUNE 13

ONE of the funny things about the stock market is that every time one person buys, another sells, and both think they are astute.

—*William Feather Sr.*

WEDNESDAY — JUNE 14

AND what is so rare as a day in June?
Then, if ever, come perfect days;
Then heaven tries earth if it be in tune,
And over it softly her warm ear lays;
Whether we look, or whether we listen,
We hear life murmur, or see it glisten,
Every clod feels a stir of might,
An instinct within it that reaches and towers
And groping blindly above it for light
Clings to a soul in grass and flowers.

—*James Russell Lowell*

THURSDAY — JUNE 15

LIVE so that your friends can defend you but never have to.

—*Arnold H. Glasgow*

THE HERITAGE BOOK

Alexander Graham Bell wrote, "I have travelled round the globe, I have seen the Canadian Rockies, the Andes, and the Highlands of Scotland. But for simple beauty, Cape Breton outrivals them all."

If you have never visited this area in Canada you have missed seeing some of our most spectacular scenery.

The 286-km Cabot Trail curves around headlands swept by the Atlantic Ocean. It edges on cliffs that drop three hundred metres to the sea and winds beside rivers between the ancient hills. The road passes through small Acadian communities such as Chéticamp, Grand Etang, and Belle Côte.

Scotland was the homeland of many of the earliest settlers in Cape Breton, and traditional ties are renewed at the Nova Scotia "Gaelic Mod," an August festival of music and dance held in St. Anns. The local Gaelic College ensures that the language and lore of the clans survive among those of Scottish ancestry.

For any of you looking to make summer travel plans, Cape Breton is breathtakingly beautiful and historically compelling.

SATURDAY — JUNE 17

MARG and Bruce had a lovely outing today. Several years ago Bruce purchased bicycles and helmets for them both and since then they have enjoyed cycling on a regular basis.

On today's trip they rode to Springridge Farm just outside Milton where they spent several hours picking strawberries.

Springridge is a large "pick your own" berry farm but it offers much more. A small restaurant serves sandwiches on homemade bread as well as fresh desserts, and a gift shop features unique arts and crafts.

Marg and Bruce enjoyed a delicious lunch before cycling home with a good supply of fresh strawberries.

This evening we'll enjoy our first strawberry shortcake of the season, so their good day has made my day as well.

SUNDAY — JUNE 18

THOU wilt make known to me the path of life; in Thy presence is fullness of joy; in Thy right hand there are pleasures forever.

—Psalm 16:11

THE HERITAGE BOOK

Monday — June 19

Fear not that thy life shall come to an end, but rather fear that it shall never have a beginning.

—Cardinal Newman

Tuesday — June 20

Be happy with what you have and are, be generous with both, and you won't have to hunt for happiness.

—William Gladstone

Wednesday — June 21

I welcome this first day of summer with open arms. I confess that as the years pass I take more and more pleasure in the warm days of this season.

Summer afternoon—summer afternoon; to me those have always been the two most beautiful words in the English language.

—Henry James

THE HERITAGE BOOK

<u>THURSDAY — JUNE 22</u>

THIS was a most enjoyable day for Marg and me. We volunteer three afternoons a week at our local school, reading to youngsters who, for whatever reason, have not been read to very often. As a result their interest in reading on their own has not been very high, and many of them are reading at a lower level than that of their classmates.

Today our "reading buddies" presented us each with a diploma announcing that we had graduated to the next grade and that we were able to move up with the class and spend time next year with many of the same students. There would be one difference, as young Jeff proudly announced. "Next year *we'll* read to *you*."

<u>FRIDAY — JUNE 23</u>

SOLVENCY is entirely a matter of temperament and not of income.

—Logan Pearsall Smith

THE HERITAGE BOOK

THE Reverend Gene Britton made this interesting point.

Next time you're feeling unimportant try this little arithmetic trick based on the fact that it took two people—your parents—to get you here. Each of your parents had two parents, so in your grandparents' generation there were four people whose love contributed to your existence.

You are a product of eight great-grandparents, sixteen great-great-grandparents, and so on. Keep on multiplying this figure by two. If you assume an average of 25 years between each generation you'll find that only 500 years ago there were 1,048,576 people on this earth beginning the production of you.

I WILL give thanks to Thee, O Lord, among the peoples; I will sing praises to Thee among the nations. For Thy loving kindness is great to the heaven, and Thy truth to the clouds. Be exalted among the heavens, O God; Let Thy glory be above all the earth.

—*Psalm 57:9-11*

Monday — June 26

PAY as little attention to discouragement as possible! Plough ahead as a steamer does, rough or smooth, rain or shine! To carry your cargo and make your port is the point.

—*M. Babcock*

Tuesday — June 27

IN every seed to breathe the flower,
In every drop of dew
To reverence a cloistered star
Within the distant blue;
To wait the promise of the bow
Despite the cloud between,
Is faith—the fervid evidence
Of loveliness unseen.

—*John B. Tabb*

Wednesday — June 28

As a music lover I appreciate Friedrich Wilhelm Nietzsche's sentiment: "Without music life would be a mistake."

THURSDAY — JUNE 29

My friend Will describes the middle years as "that quiet, peaceful, serene period between completing the children's university education and starting in to help with the first grandchildren. The middle years," he says, "usually last from three to five months."

FRIDAY — JUNE 30

A smooth sea never made a skillful mariner; neither do uninterrupted prosperity and success qualify people for usefulness and happiness.

July

Edna Jaques' poem "Stability" makes me think of home on this 128th Canada Day.

The solid fundamental things of earth
That never change no matter what the age:
Buck brush and willows by a shiny pond,
A summer morning and the smell of sage . . .

A couple, middle-aged yet finding still
The dear companionship of younger days,
A lantern hanging in a dingy barn
Making a golden circle with its rays;

A sturdy cottage on a village street,
A church door open to the passer-by,
A mother leading home a tired child,
A blue star glowing in a twilight sky;

These are the things of piety and worth
That hold together all of God's earth.

THE HERITAGE BOOK

I WILL bless the Lord at all times; his praise shall continually be in my mouth. My soul shall make its boast in the Lord; the humble shall hear it and rejoice. O magnify the Lord with me, and let us exalt His name together.

—Psalm 34:1-3

MY dear friend Marcia, a Bostonian, spends much of her summer vacation in the beautiful state of Vermont. She had this interesting story to tell me in her most recent letter.

In Waterbury, Vermont, ice cream makers Ben and Jerry have found an environmentally-friendly way to get rid of the factory's waste. Some five hundred-plus pigs are fed "ice-cream slop"—the same goop that used to go down the sewers.

Each pig eats about two gallons of the flavour of the day, and according to Ben and Jerry's they love it—especially Chocolate Chip Cookie Dough. The least popular flavour? Mint-Chocolate.

THE HERITAGE BOOK

Tuesday — July 4

Today I would like to wish a happy July 4th to all of my dear American friends. I offer you "The Colossus," the Emma Lazarus sonnet to the Bartholdi Statue of Liberty, as a most fitting tribute.

Not like the brazen giant of Greek fame,
With conquering limbs astride from land to
  land,
Here at our sea-washed, sunset gates shall
  stand
A mighty woman with a torch, whose flame
Is the imprisoned lightning, and her name
Mother of Exiles. From her beacon hand
Glows world-wide welcome; her mild eyes
  command
The air-bridged harbour that twin cities
  frame.
"Keep ancient lands, your storied pomp!" cries
  she
With silent lips. "Give me your tired, your poor,
Your huddled masses yearning to breathe free,
The wretched refuse of your teeming shore.
Send these, the homeless, tempest-tost to me,
I lift my lamp beside the golden door!"

THE HERITAGE BOOK

WEDNESDAY — JULY 5

BETTER by far you should forget and smile
Than that you should remember and
be sad.

—*Christina Rossetti*

THURSDAY — JULY 6

COMEDIAN Red Skelton used to tell his
friends that he had a terrific morning
ritual.

"You know how I get up? I open my eyes. If
I don't see flowers or smell candles I must be
alive. So I get up."

FRIDAY — JULY 7

AND pluck till time and times are done
The silver apples of the moon,
The golden apples of the sun.

—*William Butler Yeats*

Saturday — July 8

ALEXANDER, Caesar, Charlemagne and myself founded empires; but on what foundation did we rest the creations of our genius? Upon force. Jesus Christ founded an empire upon love; and at this hour millions of men would die for Him.

—Napoleon Bonaparte

Sunday — July 9

I WAITED patiently for the Lord; and He inclined to me, and heard my cry. He brought me up out of the pit of destruction, out of the miry clay; and He set my feet upon a rock making my footsteps firm.

—Psalm 40:1-2

THE HERITAGE BOOK

<u>MONDAY — JULY 10</u>

THIS is the time of year when many children are fortunate enough to be able to go to camp.

I always get a chuckle from my grandson Fred who likes to tell of campers' letters home to parents. Here are a few examples:

Dear Mom: I left home in such a hurry I think I forgot to hang up the phone. Could you please check? Love Sandy.

Dear Mom and Dad: Could you please write and tell me what an epidemic is? Love Marcie.

Dear Parents: There are 190 boys at this camp. I wish there were 189. Your loving son John.

Hi Mom and Dad: Guess what! Three girls in my cabin have direrear. I don't. Love Sandra.

TUESDAY — JULY 11

EFFORTS at recycling are paying some unexpected dividends in farming these days.

Farmers say that phone book bedding is warmer and more absorbent than the conventional straw bedding, so many dairy cows are now sleeping on shredded telephone books instead of straw. Apparently cows injure themselves less and produce more milk when their bedding is made from recycled directories.

As well, when the old bedding is tossed away it can be used as compost—and crops grown with it are flourishing. (I suppose this gives new meaning to the expression, "Your number's up.")

Isn't it wonderful to see so many people working to save the environment?

WEDNESDAY — JULY 12

FRIENDSHIP cheers like a sunbeam; charms like a good story; inspires like a brave leader; binds like a golden chain; guides like a heavenly vision.

—N. D. Hillis

THE HERITAGE BOOK

<u>Thursday — July 13</u>

A white tent pitched by a glassy lake,
Well under a shady tree,
Or by rippling rills from the grand old hills
Is the summer home for me.
I fear no blaze of the noontide rays,
For the woodland glades are mine,
The fragrant air, and that perfume rare,
The odour of forest pine.

A cooling plunge at the break of day,
A paddle, a row, or sail,
With always a fish for a mid-day dish,
And plenty of Adam's ale.
With rod or gun, or in hammock swung,
We glide through the pleasant days;
When darkness falls on our canvas walls,
We kindle the camp-fire's blaze.

From out the gloom sailed the silv'ry moon,
O'er forests dark and still,
Now far, now near, ever sad and clear,
Comes the plaint of the whip-poor-will;
With song and laugh, and with kindly chaff,
We startle the birds above,
Then rest tired heads on our cedar beds,
To dream of the ones we love.

—*Sir James Edgar*

Friday — July 14

THIS "Desiderata" was found in Old Saint Paul's Church in Baltimore, Maryland, dated 1692. Because it is much too long to include on one page I am going to divide it over several days for the next few weeks. I found the words to be as inspirational and relevant today as when they were written more than three hundred years ago.

Go placidly amid the noise and haste and remember what peace there may be in silence. As far as possible without surrender, be on good terms with all persons. Speak your truth quietly and clearly and listen to others, even the dull and ignorant; they too, have their story.

THE HERITAGE BOOK

As a senior I feel it is important to "exercise" my brain on a regular basis. People sometimes tease me, but one of the ways I like to use my little grey cells is by doing the crossword puzzle in the newspaper each day. Sometimes the puzzles are quite simple and I am able to finish in a short time. On other days, when the puzzle is more difficult, I am forced to use a dictionary, encyclopedias, the atlas, and whatever else I can find to assist me.

I usually learn something new each day, which I think is very significant for our well-being as we age. Perhaps some of you feel as I do.

Hear my cry, O God; give heed to my prayer. From the end of the earth I call to Thee, when my heart is faint; lead me to the rock that is higher than I.

—Psalm 61:1-2

MONDAY — JULY 17

AFTER reading many articles on the hazards of summer's heat and sun, I offer you some of their most important suggestions.

• Wear a suitable sunscreen. A waterproof protector with an SPF (sun protection factor) of fifteen or higher is suggested by doctors. UV rays are strongest between ten a.m. and three p.m., so prolonged exposure at this time should be avoided.

• Sunglasses with 100 percent U.V. protection should be worn whenever you are outdoors.

• Drink as much water as you can. Water keeps tissues hydrated and can prevent irritability, dizziness, and headaches.

• Avoid large meals, as they swamp your digestive system and detract from the body's ability to cool itself.

• Dress appropriately: cotton is an excellent summer material.

Most of all, enjoy the summer. People are generally healthier during this season.

TUESDAY — JULY 18

AVOID loud and aggressive persons, they are vexation to the spirit. If you compare yourself with others, you may become vain and bitter; for always there will be greater and lesser persons than yourself. Enjoy your achievements as well as your plans.

—Desiderata

WEDNESDAY — JULY 19

GENIUS is an infinite capacity for taking pains.

—Jane Ellice Hopkins

THURSDAY — JULY 20

LIFE is a mystery as deep as ever death can be;
Yet oh, how sweet it is to us, this life we live and see!

—Mary Mapes Dodge

THE HERITAGE BOOK

My friend Mavis Tewksbury, a native of Winnipeg, Manitoba, recently attended a wedding in Yorkton, Saskatchewan.

"I find this area extremely interesting, Edna. I've learned that in the nineteenth century immigrants came here from Germany, England, Scotland, Sweden, the Ukraine, and even Russia. The Russian Doukhobors, members of a pacifist religious sect, arrived here penniless in 1899. The men worked at railway construction while the women harnessed themselves to plows to work the farms.

"Here in Yorkton you can see the silver domes of the Ukrainian churches above the rooftops. In St. Mary's Ukrainian Catholic church, where we celebrated the wedding, there is a magnificent fresco on the ceiling which depicts the crowning of the Virgin Mary in heaven. This painting is stunning, Edna! It is nineteen metres in diameter and took the artist Stephen Meush three years to complete.

"I hope to stay an extra few days just to absorb some of this fascinating history."

THE HERITAGE BOOK

MANY members of our family have made a commitment to M.O.R.E., the Multiple Organ Retrieval and Exchange program that administers the province-wide computer system listing potential recipients and allocating donated organs.

At any one time there are more than seven hundred potential transplant recipients in Ontario waiting for a donated heart, lung, liver or kidneys. Yet, tragically, these transplant organs are in critically short supply.

We became aware of the program two years ago, when the nine-year-old son of good friends developed hepatitis. His condition deteriorated so quickly that he was moved to the head of the liver transplant list. Fortunately for Scott a donor was found and the lifesaving transplant was performed.

It was at that time that our family decided to carry donor cards, and since then we have told other family members and friends about this important life-saving program.

You can find out about saving lives through transplants by contacting your province's Ministry of Health.

Sunday — July 23

Truth springs from the earth; and righteousness looks down from heaven. Indeed the Lord will give what is good; and our land will yield its produce.

—Psalm 85:11-12

Monday — July 24

Keep interested in your own career, however humble; it is a real possession in the changing fortunes of time. Exercise caution in your business affairs; for the world is full of trickery. But let this not blind you to what virtue there is; many persons strive for high ideals; and everywhere life is full of heroism.

—Desiderata

Tuesday — July 25

A little girl came home from a neighbour's house where her young friend had died.
"Why did you go?" asked her father.
"To comfort her mother," replied the child.
"What were you able to do to comfort her?"
"I climbed into her lap and cried with her."

THE HERITAGE BOOK

FATHER guard me through the night,
Till the early morning light.
Give me strength to face the day,
Guide me lest my footsteps stray.

Father lead me o'er the miles,
Through life's obstacles and trials,
Teach me then to lift mine eyes
For reassurance from the skies.

Father to my mind impart
A message that will give me heart;
Gently take and hold my hand
That I obey Thy just command.

Father at the close of day
Teach my lips to quietly pray,
For once again when night is gone
Strength renewed in another dawn.
—*Margaret Jewell*

ONE big test of faith is to see others succeed-
ing financially when we are not, and then
rejoice with them.

THE HERITAGE BOOK

<u>Friday — July 28</u>

We love old cathedrals, old furniture, old silver, old dictionaries and old prints, but we have entirely forgotten about the beauty of old men. I think an appreciation of that kind of beauty is essential to our life; for beauty it seems, is what is old and mellow and well smoked.

—*Lin Yutang*

<u>Saturday — July 29</u>

Be yourself. Especially, do not feign affection. Neither be cynical about love; for in the face of all aridity and disenchantment it is perennial as the grass.

—*Desiderata*

THE HERITAGE BOOK

SUNDAY — JULY 30

ALMIGHTY God, our heavenly Father who art the author and giver of all good things, and who art merciful to us sinners beyond our deservings; Look upon us, we beseech thee, in thy loving kindness, and grant to us at this time such fair weather that we may receive the fruits of the earth in their season and learn by thy mercy to amend our lives to the glory of Thy holy Name; through Jesus Christ our Lord. Amen.

MONDAY — JULY 31

MY grandson Marshall often joins his father for a round of golf.

Their foursome last Saturday included Bob, a minister and friend of Marshall's. Before each putt Bob would say a few words to himself and then hit the ball. He began sinking putts from all over the green.

Marshall kidded, "Bob, why don't you teach me your little prayer and maybe my putts will go in too."

"Won't work!" laughed Bob. "I just tell myself to concentrate. And even if it was a prayer, you're a terrible putter!"

August

Do you pause to see the sunrise
As you start each golden day?
Do you stop to watch the sunset
In the midst of work or play?

Do you listen to another
As he shares his dreams with you?
Do you give him inspiration
For great deeds that he would do?

Do you give a cheerful greeting
To persons who are sad?
Do you reach out, smile and touch them?
Do you leave them feeling glad?

Do you give yourself in service?
Are your motives good and true?
When you spend life helping others
They will see God's love in you!

—William Arthur Ward

THE HERITAGE BOOK

WEDNESDAY — AUGUST 2

Leaves are like ideas in the mind. They come when needed. They flourish and give life, light and wisdom. When ideas have served their purpose, they need to be swept away. We must constantly sweep out the old to make way for the new.

—*Jan McKeithan*

THURSDAY — AUGUST 3

We are fortunate to have the Americans, the friendliest of neighbours, to the south of us. Canadian diplomat Hugh Keenleyside once remarked on the border that separates our two countries, calling it "a typically human creation . . . physically invisible, geographically illogical, militarily indefensible and emotionally inescapable."

FRIDAY — AUGUST 4

When a man's pursuit gradually makes his face shine and grow handsome, be sure it is a worthy one.

—*William James*

THE HERITAGE BOOK

WHAT a nice day this was! My great-grandsons Mickey and Geoffrey came to visit and I swear they have grown a foot this summer!

Both boys are working on a farm mowing, cleaning stalls, exercising horses and doing any other jobs asked of them. Mickey was particularly proud to show off the muscles that have developed in his arms.

"Do you remember how puny my arms were, Gran? Well, just look at them now." He flexed his arm and his muscles bulged surprisingly. "My friends aren't going to believe it," he crowed.

Today's conversation centred around the boys' hopes for the future. Both of them want to go on to university after completing their high school education. Geoffrey surprised me by saying that he would like very much to attend the Royal Military College in Kingston, and that he wants to earn his degree and give something back to this country by serving several years in the armed forces.

After listening to the media come down hard on today's youth it's nice to have one's faith restored—particularly when that renewed faith comes from one's own family.

Sunday — August 6

Iᶠ you do not know what there is on earth, do you expect to know what there is in heaven?
—*The Talmud*

Monday — August 7

Mᴬᴿɢ and I drove to Muskoka today where I will enjoy my annual visit with Eleanor.

On the way we stopped in Orillia, the home of one of my favourite authors, Stephen Leacock.

Explaining his attachment to the area where he spent his boyhood, Leacock wrote, "To my way of thinking, nothing will stand comparison with the smiling beauty of the waters, shores and bays of Lake Simcoe and its sister lake, Couchiching."

His lakeshore residence, built in 1928, is now a museum. On display are several of his handwritten manuscripts, and looking at his work gave me a feeling of inspiration.

Any of you contemplating a visit may wish to have it coincide with the annual Mariposa Festival in August, inspired by Leacock's most famous work, *Sunshine Sketches of a Little Town.*

THE HERITAGE BOOK

Each year I am surprised by the stunning beauty of the Muskokas. It's as if my memory isn't able to retain the loveliness and I see it anew with each visit.

At the turn of the century Algernon Blackwood, the British writer, wrote of his visit here, "The Muskoka interlude remained for me a sparkling, radiant memory, alight with the sunshine of unclouded skies, with the gleam of stars in a blue black heaven."

Although there have been changes since then the Muskoka air is still crystal clear and the landscape remains largely unchanged. It is now, as it was then, a magnet that draws cottagers back year after year to enjoy its magnificence.

THE HERITAGE BOOK

TAKE kindly the counsel of the years, gracefully surrendering the things of youth. Nurture strength of spirit to shield you in sudden misfortune. But do not distress yourself with imaginings. Many fears are born of fatigue and loneliness. Beyond a wholesome discipline, be gentle with yourself.

—Desiderata

YOUTH is not a time of life—it is a state of mind.

Nobody grows old by merely living a number of years; people grow old by deserting their ideals. Years wrinkle the skin, but to give up enthusiasm wrinkles the soul. Worry, doubt, self-distrust, fear and despair . . . these are the long, long years that bow the head and turn the growing spirit back to dust.

THE HERITAGE BOOK

FRIDAY — AUGUST 11

THIS morning Eleanor found some very old newspapers in a long-forgotten trunk in a cupboard. The papers are from 1945. As I was reading I came upon the following advertisement:

"Bala Bay Lodge at Bala, Ontario. Direct C.P.R. We meet all trains. Muskoka's famous red brick hotel. 66 Rooms, hot, cold running water in each room; city conveniences; unexcelled sleeping comforts; delicious meals, planned entertainment; dancing, all sports facilities. Write direct LA 3691 or LA 9085."

How interesting it was to drive past this lodge today. Although the name is now "The Cranberry House" one could well imagine it as it was fifty summers ago.

SATURDAY — AUGUST 12

PEACE and joy
And love and warmth
And happiness
Throughout the nation
Summer Vacation.

—Shelley Silverstein

THE HERITAGE BOOK

GIVE thanks to the God of heaven, for His loving kindness is everlasting.

—*Psalm 136:26*

ACCORDING to geologists the rock in Muskoka is the oldest on earth.

One of the most impressive displays of this rock is the cut on Highway 118 about ten miles north of Bracebridge. Blasted out to make way for the highway, it is a half mile long and forty feet high. In some places the rock is so smooth it looks knife-sliced.

The dazzling pink rock so impressed Dorothy Duke of the boat-building Port Carling family that when she saw it she "wanted to stop the car, jump on the hood and sing 'O Canada' at the top of my lungs."

TUESDAY — AUGUST 15

FOR there is no friend like a sister
In calm or stormy weather;
To cheer one on the tedious way,
To fetch one if one goes astray,
To lift one if one totters down,
To strengthen whilst one stands.

—*Christina Rossetti*

WEDNESDAY — AUGUST 16

TIME is a versatile performer. It flies, marches on, heals all wounds, runs out, and will tell.

THURSDAY — AUGUST 17

OF all good gifts which ever came out of the wallet of the Fairy Godmother, the gift of natural gladness is the greatest and best. It is to the soul what health is to the body, what sanity is to the mind, the test of normality.

—*Bliss Carman*

THE HERITAGE BOOK

THIS evening Eleanor and I sat in our old wooden Muskoka chairs out under the stars.

I think what I enjoy most in the north is the peace that comes at nightfall. Tonight as we sat in the stillness a mother deer and her two fawn wandered out of the woods, grazing at the edge of the forest. They didn't seem at all worried by our presence, and wandered quietly for some time before heading back into the trees.

A loon's call broke the silence and from down the bay we heard the answering cry. Very soon both of the birds swam into view, just visible in the twilight.

As darkness fell and the stars began to twinkle I said a silent prayer of thanks for the good health that has allowed me to enjoy so many of these memorable evenings.

GOD loves an idling rainbow
No less than labouring seas.
—*Ralph Hodgson*

THE HERITAGE BOOK

O LORD, support us all day long, until the shadows lengthen and the evening comes, and the busy world is hushed, and the fever of life is over and our work is done. Then in thy mercy grant us a safe lodging, and a holy rest, and peace at last.

—Book of Common Prayer

No matter how much we enjoy a holiday there is something special about coming home. These few lines came back to me as I savoured my morning tea.

So I set off when gypsy blood
Wells up and urges me to start,
I wander on and on until
Homesickness strikes my heart.

World travel has its golden days
And it is nice at times to roam,
But far the best part of adventure:
Return to Home Sweet Home.

THE HERITAGE BOOK

MARG and I noticed something very interesting in a magazine today. An advertisement for children's fall clothing was noteworthy, not for the styles of clothes, but for the youngsters modelling them. This is the first time I have seen models who are Down syndrome children. And one little girl was physically disabled and in a special wheelchair.

Perhaps nowhere else have the young and visually perfect reigned more supreme than in the world of fashion modelling. Yet the world is by no means young and "perfect"; it is of course quite the opposite.

It would seem that in our country where we embrace different cultures, skin colours, sizes, ages, the able-bodied and the physically and mentally challenged, consumers would demand reality in advertising.

Maybe the ad we saw today is the beginning of a welcome change in this industry.

THE past cannot be changed; the future is still in your power.

THE HERITAGE BOOK

My grandson Fred and his wife June returned from holidays today. As Fred remarked, "The marvellous thing about a vacation is that it makes you feel good enough to go back to work and poor enough to make you have to."

You are a child of the universe, no less than the trees and the stars; you have a right to be here. And whether or not it is clear to you, no doubt the universe is unfolding as it should.
—*Desiderata*

No one should make such thorough preparation for the rainy days that he or she can't enjoy today's sunshine.

THE HERITAGE BOOK

SUNDAY — AUGUST 27

ALMIGHTY God, unto whom all hearts be open, all desires known, and from whom no secrets are hid; cleanse the thoughts of our hearts by the inspiration of thy Holy Spirit, that we may perfectly love thee, and worthily magnify thy Holy Name; through Jesus Christ, our Lord, Amen.

—Book of Common Prayer

MONDAY — AUGUST 28

THE best and most beautiful things in the world cannot be seen or even touched. They must be felt with the heart.

—Helen Keller

TUESDAY — AUGUST 29

ONE's life has value so long as one attributes value to the life of others, by means of love, friendship, indignation and compassion.

—Simone de Beauvoir

THE HERITAGE BOOK

Our neighbour Pat had this very funny story for us today.

Last night Pat's husband Roger, after a long day at the office, decided to have a leisurely bath to unwind. As usual Barclay, their young yellow Labrador, lay in the hall outside the bathroom door "guarding" his master.

To make her mother happy, their daughter Karen decided to vacuum her carpet. Much to Barclay's distress (the dog having a distinct loathing for the vacuum cleaner) Karen turned on the machine.

In his fright the seventy-pound animal leaped at the bathroom door, sending it flying open, and hurled himself into the bathtub landing right on top of a very surprised Roger. Man and dog thrashed about until Roger was finally able to get out from under the terrified Barclay and exit the tub.

Roger and Barclay are fine, and Karen and Pat still laugh just thinking about it.

The more you know, the more you know you don't know.

September

SEPTEMBER has arrived bringing with it a return to school as well as the first signs of autumn. These lovely lines from Marion Doyle remind us of the beauty of the coming season.

See what a riot of colour!
Hark, what a riot of sound!
Golden grain and golden leaves
Rustling on the ground.

Here is a wealth worth hoarding,
Here is the gold of God!
The sun upon the harvest fields,
And the gleam of goldenrod.

THE HERITAGE BOOK

THIS is the last Saturday before children return to schools all across the country. Many parents are flocking to the malls to buy much-needed new clothing for their young ones who have "shot up" over the summer months. As well, school supplies—pencil crayons, backpacks, paper, etc. are much sought-after items.

The twins, Justin and Jenny, went shopping with their parents today for the things they'll need.

I find it interesting to see the differences in their personalities. Jenny, the quieter and calmer of the two, takes a great interest in all of their purchases. She looks carefully at each item and much thought goes into her selections. Justin can hardly bear to take the time to glance at his choices.

"Oh sure—whatever—that's fine," are the expressions he uses as Phyllis tries to get him to choose some clothing.

"Gran, I swear he'd wear any old thing just so that he didn't have to spend time shopping."

I guess this is what makes our world so wonderful. Two children, twins, raised by the same parents and yet so different, can be loved equally dearly.

THE HERITAGE BOOK

Great and marvellous are Thy works, O Lord God the Almighty; Righteous and true are Thy ways, Thou King of the nations.
—Revelation 15:3

Labour Day

On this last long weekend of the summer I have enjoyed seeing many of the young people return to the neighbourhood from summer jobs out of the area.

In the tough economic times that our country has experienced in the past years summer jobs for students have been increasingly difficult to find.

John, a university student in our area, talked with me about this problem.

"The scarcity of jobs isn't altogether a bad thing. Those of us lucky enough to find a job knew there were ten people waiting to take our places if we didn't work hard. If we are to have any hope of getting into our chosen field we must strive to be the very best we can be!"

Hard times can provide good lessons.

THE HERITAGE BOOK

For most of the students in our province this is the first day of school. How I love to watch the children decked out in their "first day" finery as they make their way to class.

Christie, who is a close friend of my grand-daughter Phyllis, teaches grade one students and recently shared her hopes with me.

"This year will be a big challenge. In my class I have two 'special needs' students, a little boy who is profoundly deaf and a little girl who has spina bifida and is in a wheelchair. I want to be sure that the rest of the children and I do our very best to be sure that we work together as a group, with no one member being treated any differently from another."

I know that if anyone can do this job exceptionally well it is Christie. Today I offered a special prayer, not just for Christie, but for all teachers who are entrusted with our greatest resources, the minds of the young.

Joy is a net of love by which you can catch souls.

—Mother Teresa

THE HERITAGE BOOK

O NATURE! I do not aspire
To be the highest in thy choir—
To be a meteor in thy sky,
Or comet that may range on high;
Only a zephyr that may blow
Among the reeds by the river low;
Give me thy most privy place
Where to run my airy race.

In some withdrawn, unpublic mead
Let me sigh upon a reed,
Or in the woods, with leafy din,
Whisper the still evening in:
Some still work give me to do—
Only—be it near to you!

For I'd rather be thy child
And pupil, in the forest wild,
Than be the king of men elsewhere,
And most sovereign slave of care;
To have one moment of thy dawn,
Than share the city's year forlorn.

—*Henry David Thoreau*

FRIDAY — SEPTEMBER 8

LIFE is the first gift, love is the second and understanding the third.

—*Marge Piercy*

SATURDAY — SEPTEMBER 9

TODAY Marg and I took a drive in the country. As we were passing a farm a large handprinted sign at the side of the road caught our attention. We pulled over to the stand at the driveway's end and admired the assortment of fresh produce. Although no one was there, a note read "Please help yourself. The tin for the money is on the shelf. Thank you."

This evening we made a meal out of those lovely fresh vegetables and some homemade bread. As well as enjoying our dinner, I felt very good about the fact that there are still people who trust in the honesty of others.

SUNDAY — SEPTEMBER 10

THE Lord is in His holy temple: let all the earth keep silent before Him.

—*Habakkuk 2:20*

THE HERITAGE BOOK

Many friends and readers have asked if there is any secret to the good health I have enjoyed throughout my life. In truth I do believe there are a few common-sense things that may help you stay healthy, but on the whole, I think it depends on good luck rather than on good management.

Except for hereditary diseases, who can know why one person falls ill and not another? Why are some cured and not others?

In my advancing years I have tried to eat well, maintain a healthy weight, drink a lot of water, and exercise every day.

I'm sure that this regimen helps me to stay healthy, but I think I have probably had more than my share of good luck as well.

The giving of love is an education in itself.

—Eleanor Roosevelt

THE HERITAGE BOOK

As Lila and I passed the high school on our walk today we saw a sure sign of autumn. Out on the field were about fifty young men in football gear running, throwing the ball, tackling one another, or doing drills. No doubt they were trying to impress the coach—hoping to earn a place in the starting lineup for the season.

My late husband George used to love watching football, and for several years he helped out as a high school coach.

George's approach to coaching was not a very orthodox one by most people's standards. For he put a lot of stock in effort and attitude, and the boys soon learned that if they didn't give their all in a practice they spent a lot of time on the bench.

On several occasions parents were critical of George's methods, but as the boys came to understand how George coached the parents too seemed to learn that effort and a positive attitude earned just as much success as athletic brilliance.

The boys learned a lesson in life as well as in football.

THE HERITAGE BOOK

My friend Marion, who is a secretary at a law firm, passed along this amusing look at a secretary's day.

A. M.
"He hasn't come in yet."
"I expect him any moment."
"He's just sent word that he'll be a little late."
"He's been in but he's gone out again."
"He's gone to lunch."

P. M.
"I expect him back any minute."
"He hasn't come back yet. May I take a message?"
"He's somewhere in the building."
"Yes he was in, but he went out again."
"I don't know whether he'll be back or not."
"No, he's gone for the day."

The only thing heavier than carrying a chip on your shoulder is carrying a grudge in your heart.

THE HERITAGE BOOK

Hold fast to dreams
For if dreams die
Like a broken-winged bird
They cannot flie.

—Langston Hughes

I thought you might enjoy a few interesting facts about the Bible today.

The Bible contains 733,746 words, 31,163 verses, 1,189 chapters, and 66 books. The longest chapter is the 119th Psalm and the shortest is the 117th Psalm. The Bible contains two testaments; the Old is Law, the New is Love. In the Old, humanity is reaching up for God. In the New, God is reaching down for humanity.

The Bible is the most widely read book ever published.

Knowledge comes from taking things apart but wisdom comes from putting things together.

THE HERITAGE BOOK

To be happy at home is the ultimate aim of all ambition; the end to which every enterprise and labour tends, and of which every desire prompts the prosecution.
—*Samuel Johnson*

IT's right to be contented with what you have but never with what you are.

THEY talk of the days that are rare in June;
They sing of the beauties of spring;
They tell of the gleaming in the white winter's snow
They write of what each season brings.

But give me a day in Autumn rare
When Indian Summer is here—
The days are so hot and the nights so cool
And the air is so radiantly clear.
—*Edna Horvath*

FRIDAY — SEPTEMBER 22

Opinions that are well rooted should grow and change like a healthy tree.

SATURDAY — SEPTEMBER 23

Today we enjoyed a family outing to the first of the many fall fairs in our area. The nice thing about these fairs is that there are things to enjoy for all age groups. The youngsters loved the farm animal exhibits, especially the sheep-shearing exhibition. Marg and Bruce liked the woodworking and handicraft displays, while I marvelled at the handiwork of the quilts.

We all ate heartily in the food tent, where Octoberfest sausages, mounds of mashed potatoes, corn, tomatoes, and homemade pies made up our delicious dinner meal.

If you've never attended a fair it provides a most enjoyable outing.

SUNDAY — SEPTEMBER 24

And I said "O that I had wings like a dove! I would fly away and be at rest."

—Psalm 55:6

THE HERITAGE BOOK

ONE is never so brilliant as when one takes the words right out of your mouth.

GROWING old is no more than a bad habit which a busy person has no time to form.

I AM always content with that which happens, for I think that which God chooses is better than what I choose.

—Epictetus

LOST wealth may be replaced by industry, lost knowledge by study, lost health by temperance, but lost time is gone forever.

THE HERITAGE BOOK

I WAS interested to learn that some of the "ordinary technologies" we take for granted today were originally developed for the American space program launched in 1958.

According to NASA officials more than 30,000 life-saving or life-improving products have come into our lives as a result of a need within the space program.

Smoke detectors, a standard feature in almost every home, were developed from a smoke detector created for use on Skylab.

Fire fighters' breathing apparatus came as a direct application of the Apollo backpack life support system. Fire fighters using these tanks have reduced by ninety percent the need for hospitalization from smoke inhalation.

Computer technology advanced more quickly because of NASA's demands on the industry.

Cordless tools are a result of the need for battery-powered tools used on moon landings.

The world of medicine has benefited as well. High-tech heart rate monitors evolved out of the need to monitor astronauts during flight; and technology used in the Lunar Rover now allows quadriplegics to drive cars.

It seems that we all are indebted to NASA.

THE HERITAGE BOOK

I WANT, by understanding myself, to understand others. I want to be all that I am capable of becoming.... This all sounds very strenuous and serious. But now that I have wrestled with it, it's no longer so. I feel happy—deep down. *All is well.*

—*Katherine Mansfield*

COURAGE is the price that life exacts for granting peace.
The soul that knows it not, knows no release
From little things;
Knows not the livid loneliness of fear,
Nor mountain heights where bitter joy can hear
The sound of wings.

—*Amelia Earhart*

October

O<small>N</small> this first Sunday of October I offer part of Dean Alford's hymn of thanks for a wonderful harvest.

Come, ye thankful people, come.
Raise the song of harvest home!
All is safely gathered in
Ere the winter storm begins:
God, our Maker, doth provide
For our wants to be supplied:
Come to God's own temple, come,
Raise the song of harvest home.

THE HERITAGE BOOK

MONDAY — OCTOBER 2

THE right word may be effective, but no word was ever as effective as a rightly timed pause.

—*Mark Twain*

TUESDAY — OCTOBER 3

WE all know that books burn—yet we have the greater knowledge that books cannot be killed by fire. People die, but books can never die. No man and no force can abolish memory.

—*Franklin D. Roosevelt*

WEDNESDAY — OCTOBER 4

A YOUNG lad in our neighbourhood drives a very old, rather bashed-about small car. He didn't realize just how bad it looked until one evening when he pulled over to the curb and got out to check a tire. A passerby stopped her car and rushed over to ask if he'd been hurt in the accident.

THE HERITAGE BOOK

The true cost of a thing is the amount of what I call "life" which is required to be exchanged for it immediately or in the long run.

—Henry David Thoreau

A little more than two years ago the world lost one of its finest young people. Jonathan Bain, the grandson of dear friends, passed away suddenly just a few days after his fourteenth birthday. He died at the Hospital for Sick Children after only a three-week illness.

Jonathan was a wonderful free spirit. He was a computer "nut," skilled far beyond his years, and a ski racer dedicated to excellence.

He was a young lad you couldn't help but love—impish and fun-loving—and a wonderful son and grandson of whom the family was so proud.

Although we can never make sense of such a tragic death we can remember the great joy and happiness that he brought to so many and feel a small measure of comfort.

THE HERITAGE BOOK

THIS poem by John Gillespie McGee Jr. has long been one of my favourites. I hope it brings joy to your day.

High Flight

Oh! I have slipped the surly bonds of earth
And danced the skies on laughter-silvered
   wings,
Sunward I've climbed, and joined the
   tumbling mirth
Of sun-split clouds—and done a hundred
   things
You have not dreamed of—wheeled and
   soared and swung
High in the sunlit silence. Hov'ring there
I've chased the shouting wind along, and flung
My eager craft through footless halls of air.
Up, up the long delirious burning blue,
I've topped the windswept heights with easy
   grace
Where never lark, or even eagle flew—
And, while the silent lifting wind I've trod
The high untrespassed sanctity of space,
Put out my hand and touched the face of God.

THE HERITAGE BOOK

ALMIGHTY God we give thee humble and hearty thanks for thy goodness and loving kindness to us and all men. We thank thee for the light of thy Gospel, the labours of thy servants and the ministrations of thy Church. Amen.

Thanksgiving Day

FOR me, Thanksgiving is one of the loveliest holidays of the year. The leaves are at their most beautiful colouring, fruits and vegetables are at their delicious best, and our family gathers from far and wide to give thanks together.

This year we have a very special reason to be thankful. My grandson Marshall and his wife Jamie welcomed a son into their family fold.

Michael James came into the world early this morning, and he will be much loved and adored by us all.

THE HERITAGE BOOK

TUESDAY — OCTOBER 10

A MEMORY without blot or contamination must be an exquisite treasure, an inexhaustible source of pure refreshment.

—*Charlotte Brontë*

WEDNESDAY — OCTOBER 11

THERE are always two goals for everything we do... to get there and to enjoy the journey.

THURSDAY — OCTOBER 12

I SAW my newest great-grandchild for the first time today. How quickly we forget the tiny size of a newborn baby!

As I gazed at this small and perfect creature I couldn't help but marvel at the way families continue. This beautiful little boy is the product of many, many generations and old photographs are likely to show a resemblance to family members long departed.

It truly is miraculous, isn't it, how life goes on?

Friday — October 13

THE purpose of education is to provide everyone with the opportunity to learn how he or she may best serve the world.

Saturday — October 14

As I watched the baseball playoffs today I remembered the game between the Toronto Blue Jays and the Cleveland Indians in August '93 which marked the return of Bob Ojeda as a starting pitcher with the Indians.

Ojeda had suffered devastating injuries in a boating accident during spring training. Two other pitchers and teammates of Ojeda were killed in the accident.

Although his physical injuries were life-threatening, it was the mental anguish that almost finished Ojeda's career. It took months of therapy and encouragement from many sides before he was ready to resume his pitching.

Finally, in front of 25,000 fans who started cheering as soon as he walked on the field, he returned to the game he loved. It was an act of courage that still stirs my emotions two years later.

THE HERITAGE BOOK

SUNDAY — OCTOBER 15

FOR this is the will of my Father, that every one who beholds the Son, and believes in Him, may have eternal life; and I Myself will raise him up on the last day.

—John 6:40

MONDAY — OCTOBER 16

GRATEFUL for our festive harvest,
Blest in golden fruit and precious grain.

Grateful for rich peaceful fields,
Blest from falling rain.

Grateful for pathways leading home,
Blest in love to each his own.

Grateful for those we love so much,
Blest and created from Thy sacred touch.

Grateful for chapels to worship in prayer,
Blest in freedom beyond compare.

Grateful beyond these gifts sublime,
We are blest most of all—
For Thy precious Love sublime.

Tuesday — October 17

THEREFORE be at peace with God, whatever you conceive Him to be, and whatever your labours and aspirations, in the noisy confusion of life keep peace with your soul. With all its sham drudgery and broken dreams, it is still a beautiful world. Be careful. Strive to be happy.

—Desiderata

Wednesday — October 18

GRANDCHILDREN are the dots that connect the lines from generation to generation.

—Lois Wyse

Thursday — October 19

I AM certain of nothing but the holiness of the heart's affections and the truth of imagination—what the imagination seizes as beauty must be truth—whether it existed before or not.

—John Keats

THE HERITAGE BOOK

FRIDAY — OCTOBER 20

THE finest inheritance you can give to a child is to allow her to make her own way, completely on her own feet.

—*Isadora Duncan*

SATURDAY — OCTOBER 21

A WELL-BALANCED life is one which fails to give you what you ask for about as often as it fails to give you what you deserve.

—*F. Walsh*

SUNDAY — OCTOBER 22

THOU hast crowned the year with Thy bounty, and Thy paths drip with fatness.
The pastures of the wilderness drip, and the hills gird themselves with rejoicing.
The meadows are clothed with flocks
And the valleys are covered with grain; they shout for joy, yes, they sing.

—*Psalm 65:11-13*

THE HERITAGE BOOK

ON the radio this morning I heard an amusing observation: "When the going gets tough, the tough clean closets."

The reason I find this funny is that whenever anything unsettling occurs in our family this is exactly what happens.

When my father passed away, my mother responded to her grief by cleaning cupboards, drawers, floors, etc. She knew that cleaning and polishing would fill up a great deal of time and help to keep her mind off her sorrow.

I didn't really understand how this worked until my own husband George passed away. After his death I took the house apart from top to bottom at least five times. The more I did the more my grief seemed to ebb.

When Bruce lost his job many years ago, Marg and I both cleaned cupboards until he found a new position.

This ritual is not limited to the women of the family. If Bruce has a problem he can often be found in the basement straightening his tools.

I don't know how it works in other families, but in ours, "when the going gets tough, we clean closets."

TUESDAY — OCTOBER 24

Is there anything more lovely than an autumn drive in the country?

My friends and I in the seniors program enjoyed a delightful bus tour today. We journeyed to the Kitchener-Waterloo area and then north through the beautiful little towns of St. Jacobs, Elmira, Elora, and Fergus before returning home.

Along with the magnificent foliage we saw The Meeting Place, a museum in St. Jacobs designed to help visitors understand Mennonite history, lifestyle, and beliefs. In Elora we walked down into the Gorge and were enthralled by the incredible colours atop the steep rock cliffs.

Season of mists and mellow fruitfulness,
Close bosom-friend of the maturing sun.
—*John Keats*

WEDNESDAY — OCTOBER 25

People who know how to laugh at themselves will never cease to be amused.

THE HERITAGE BOOK

O suns and skies and clouds of June,
And flowers of June together,
Ye cannot rival for one hour
 October's bright blue weather.
                              —*Helen Hunt Jackson*

SEEK to find the best in the worst, to discover the great in the small, to see beauty in the plain, and to detect the elegant in the simple.
                              —*William Arthur Ward*

"GRAMPA" Bruce enjoyed a happy day with Justin, Jenny, and Bethany. He took them to a local farm to select pumpkins for Halloween.

"What I love best about being a grandparent is that I have a wonderful time with the children—and when they become tired or cranky someone takes them home and I am left to enjoy my memories."

THE HERITAGE BOOK

AND I saw a new heaven and a new earth; for the first heaven and the first earth passed away, and there was no longer any sea. And I saw the holy city, new Jerusalem, coming down out of heaven from God, made ready as a bride adorned for her husband.

—Revelation 21:1-2

A SMALL trouble is like a pebble. Hold it too close to your eye, and it fills the whole world and puts everything out of focus. Hold it at proper viewing distance, and it can be examined and properly classified. Throw it at your feet, and it can be seen in its true setting, just one more tiny bump on the pathway to eternity.

—C. Luce

THE HERITAGE BOOK

HALLOWEEN is a day that I really enjoy. When I see all the little people in their costumes it brings back a flood of memories—not only of Halloween with our three girls but of a time even longer ago when I was a child.

I often spent Halloween at the home of my friend Edith. Her mother would invite all the youngsters in our area to their home where she had many kinds of "horrors" in store for us.

In their basement Mrs. Parnell set up a kind of maze that we would walk through. There were white sheet "ghosts," black witches that "flew" on threads, and pans of spaghetti "innards" to put our hands in.

Upstairs we bobbed for apples in a big tub of water, and then we enjoyed homemade ice cream and cake.

Now that I look back on those wonderful nights I can see how a vivid imagination and a love of children sparked Edith's mother to provide us with such an abundance of memories.

November

All Saints Day

Every morning compose your soul for a tranquil day, and all through it be careful often to recall your resolution, and bring yourself back to it, so to say. If something discomposes you, do not be upset, or troubled; but having discovered the fact, humble yourself gently before God, and try to bring your mind into a quiet attitude. Say to yourself, "Well, I have made a false step; now I must go more carefully and watchfully." Do this each time, however frequently you fall. When you are at peace use it profitably, making constant acts of meekness, and seeking to be calm even in the most trifling things. Above all, do not be discouraged; be patient; wait; strive to attain a calm, gentle spirit.

—*St. François de Sales*

THE HERITAGE BOOK

<u>THURSDAY — NOVEMBER 2</u>

Losing everything isn't really that terrible. When you have nothing you are free.

<u>FRIDAY — NOVEMBER 3</u>

THE best preacher is the heart; the best teacher is time; the best book is the world; the best friend is God.

—The Talmud

<u>SATURDAY — NOVEMBER 4</u>

O GOD, give us the serenity to accept what cannot be changed, courage to change what should be changed, and wisdom to distinguish the one from the other.

—Reinhold Niebuhr

THE HERITAGE BOOK

At this morning's service we said this special prayer for one of the children in the parish who has been extremely ill. I hope it was a comfort to her parents.

O Lord Jesus Christ, who lovest little children and thyself didst live as a child upon earth; make her to know and feel that thou art ever near; help her to be meek and gentle, patient and obedient, and lead her to love thee more and more; restore her to health and strength, if it be thy gracious will, that she may live for thee, to the glory of thy holy Name; who livest and reignest with the Father and the Holy Ghost, one God world without end. Amen.

A good friend remarked after a recent hospital stay that he found it very educational. He learned that he wasn't covered by his insurance—or his hospital gown.

THE HERITAGE BOOK

Early this evening we took a drive to the local flying club. We enjoyed watching the sailplanes as they soared on air drafts over the local farms, up over the escarpment, and back again to land on the grass. It really was exciting to see.

Several years ago Bruce took us to an air show where we were treated to an incredible performance by Oscar Boesch in his sailplane "Wings of Man." Boesch executed a series of complex maneouvres to the music of "Born Free" and the moving words of John G. McGee, "Oh, I have slipped the surly bonds of earth . . . ."

For about eight minutes the craft looped, rolled, and flew upside-down, with each maneouvre somehow matching the mood and rhythm of the music. At one point the "Wings of Man" dropped progressively from three thousand feet—until it flew right across in front of us at an incredible speed and in complete silence.

"Every flight," said Boesch, "is a highlight. It is praise to God and an appreciation of nature."

THE HERITAGE BOOK

"AGE is simply a case of mind over matter. If you don't mind, it doesn't matter." For many of us more mature folks these words of Jack Benny's aren't a wisecrack: they are a philosophy.

Friends of mine who eat well, exercise regularly, and keep up their contacts with friends seem to feel better and enjoy life more.

Growing older isn't always easy but a positive attitude is a tremendous asset to many. If you've been feeling older lately maybe you need to try a little "mind over matter."

MARG picked up some lovely cranberry muffins at the bakery this morning and was given thirteen on her order of a dozen.

I often wondered where the expression "a baker's dozen" came from. Here is what I found out. During the Middle Ages, English bakers were heavily fined for shortchanging customers. To avoid the fines, cautious bakers began the practice of adding a free roll to the order of a dozen, making thirteen.

DARE to be brave, dare to stand tall;
Give life the best, get up when you fall.
—William Arthur Ward

SATURDAY — NOVEMBER 11

THIS prayer was printed in the *Toronto Daily Star* on May 7, 1945, on the occasion of the surrender of Germany in the Second World War.

We offer praise to God for this great day, our jubilation tempered by the memory of those gallant men and women who have laid down their lives on the Altar of Freedom ... the memory of their loved ones ... and those to whom this bitter conflict has brought sorrow and suffering.

With steadfast faith and unflinching purpose, let us fight on until God's sweet earth is completely freed from oppression and intolerance.

Let us pray the greater Guidance, which has led us to this day of triumph, shall lead us on now—swiftly—to Total Victory and Lasting Peace.

W E all, with open face beholding as in a mirror the glory of the Lord, are changed into the same image from glory to glory, even as by the Spirit of the Lord.

—II Corinthians 3:18

A PERSON'S own good manners are the best security against the rudeness of others.

—Larry Wayne

A s a lover of music it was not surprising to me when a recent study showed that background music played in a doctor's office helps to relax patients.

When classical music was played during more than one hundred consultations, eighty-three percent of patients claimed that the music reduced their stress. Sixty-seven percent said that it had helped with the consultation. Doctors take note!

THE HERITAGE BOOK

THE goldenrod is yellow,
The harvest moon is mellow,
Northern lights adorn the midnight sky.
The maple leaves are falling,
The wild grey goose is calling,
Winter's nigh.
—*Margaret Jewell*

American Thanksgiving

FOR rest and shelter of the night,
Father we thank Thee.
For health and food, and love and friends,
For everything thy goodness sends,
Father in heaven, we thank Thee.
—*Ralph Waldo Emerson*

ITSELF—its Sovereign—of itself
The Soul should stand in awe.
—*Emily Dickinson*

THE HERITAGE BOOK

A DIFFICULT decision facing those of us who are elderly is whether or not we should continue to drive.

A car offers freedom and independence that no well-meaning family member or taxi service can replace. For many elderly people the feeling of control over their lives that having an automobile can give is very important.

When should one give up driving, then? The answer to this question is difficult at best.

In most provinces drivers over eighty must be tested annually. For some drivers the test is no problem; for others eighty is much too late since their skills have been below standard well before the time of testing.

Children who feel that an aging parent shouldn't be driving may suggest to the family doctor that he or she broach the subject. Any physician who knows of an illness or disease that impairs driving must inform the Department of Transport and the licence will be suspended. In other cases a doctor will suggest a test be done to determine competency.

Safe driving is so important that we hope everyone can be realistic about their own abilities.

THE HERITAGE BOOK

Behold I tell you a mystery; we shall not all sleep, but we shall all be changed, in a moment, in a twinkling of an eye, at the last trumpet; for the last trumpet will sound, and the dead will be raised imperishable, and we shall be changed. For this perishable must put on the imperishable and this mortal must put on immortality.

—*I Corinthians 15:51-53*

Monday — November 20

Most of us who are seniors have widowed friends who have chosen a new partner and remarried. Remarriage is not for everyone, but studies have shown that widowed partners have a strong chance of success.

A good friend of mine, Marie Thomas, recently took a widower as her second husband. She and Dave are very enthusiastic about their marriage.

"Neither of us wanted to grow old alone or be a burden to our families. We are having a wonderful time together."

I hope they enjoy many happy years of wedded bliss!

TUESDAY — NOVEMBER 21

I WENT to the woods because I wished to live deliberately, to front only the essential facts of life, and see if I could not learn what it had to teach, and not, when I came to die, discover that I had not lived.

—*Henry David Thoreau*

WEDNESDAY — NOVEMBER 22

I T was on this date in 1963 that the thirty-fifth President of the United States, John F. Kennedy, was assassinated in Dallas, Texas.

The Kennedy years were an era when young men were in charge of Presidential institutions. In his inaugural address, the President noted that a new generation was coming into power. He was the first President born in the twentieth century, and he filled the chief posts with men in their thirties and forties. He described his administration as the "New Frontier."

Although his image has been severely tarnished in the years after his death, he was for a short time revered as a well-poised, rational and resolute leader both at home and in the eyes of the world.

THE HERITAGE BOOK

I HAVE somewhere met with the epitaph of a charitable man which has pleased me very much. I cannot recollect the words, but here is the sense of it:

"What I spent, I lost; what I possessed is left to others; what I gave away remains with me."
—*Joseph Addison*

IT was a delightful visit—perfect, in being much too short.

—*Jane Austen*

DR. Norman Vincent Peale, author of the best-selling book *The Power of Positive Thinking,* suggested that you can have a successful and satisfying life if you adopt these seven values. See if you agree with him. Courage. Integrity. Love. Hope. Faith. Happiness. Enthusiasm.

THE HERITAGE BOOK

SUNDAY — NOVEMBER 26

I WILL sing to the Lord as long as I live, all my life I will sing psalms to my God. May my meditation please the Lord; as for me, I shall be glad in the Lord.

—Psalm 104:33-34

MONDAY — NOVEMBER 27

How glad I was to have a fire crackling in the fireplace this evening. Today's icy chill was a reminder that winter is just around the corner.

When the days in November are cold and dreary I find that nothing cheers me more than a hot cup of tea, a good book, and a comfortable chair in front of a blazing fire. Candles burning add that special touch to make a perfect setting for a perfect evening.

When north winds are blowing and snow fills the air,
There's nothing more cozy or lovely to share
Than a big roaring fire . . . some well-chosen friends,
And the hearty welcome a fireside extends.

THE HERITAGE BOOK

ONE of the finest advances in medicine is the surgical replacement of hip and knee joints. At this time between 200,000 and 300,000 Canadians have benefited from artificial hips and knees.

My good friend Martha Kennedy has had both of her knees and one hip replaced over the past five years. She had been plagued by crippling osteoarthritis that especially affected her knees.

To remedy the pain and regain her mobility she chose the surgery that has restored her life to its once energetic style.

Replacements are made from either stainless steel or titanium, depending on which metal better serves the need of the patient.

The surgical procedure itself takes only ninety minutes and the patient is often walking, with some help, on the fourth or fifth day after surgery. In about three months they are walking with canes.

For people who have suffered from arthritis or who have joints that are just plain worn out, artificial joints offer a second chance at an active life.

THE HERITAGE BOOK

THE future is the time when you'll wish you'd done what you aren't doing now.

IT is not so much the being exempt from faults, as having overcome them, that is an advantage to us; it being with the follies of the mind as much as with the weeds of the field, which if destroyed and consumed upon the place of their birth, enrich and improve it more than if none had sprung there before.

—Alexander Pope

December

Yesterday hills and woods were grey,
And boughs were bare and brown
But all last night silently, silently
Snow came down.

All night long over the fields,
Quiet and soft and slow,
With never a footprint steadily, steadily
Walked the snow.

Now at dawn there is nothing but snow,
Nothing but whiteness now
Except the flame of a redbird's wing
On a feathery bough.

Never a sound in all the land;
Pure silence through and through,
Save for the chatter of chickadees
Debating what to do.

—Nancy Byrd Turner

THE HERITAGE BOOK

T<small>HIS</small> is a very busy time of year as shoppers scurry from store to store and mall to mall. The radio announces at regular intervals that "there are only ___ shopping days left until Christmas" and these words can strike fear in the hearts of those last-minute gift buyers.

Because I dislike the hustle and bustle of crowded shopping centres I usually make my gift selections very early—often in the summer or fall months—just to avoid the "Christmas rush."

This leaves me with plenty of time to engage in my favourite of Christmas chores: the writing of letters and cards to my many friends and relatives who live a distance away.

Because of the high cost of long-distance phone calls this is sometimes the only way that I am able to keep in touch with my far-away friends. I enjoy receiving cards and letters so much that I try to make those I send as interesting and fun to read as I can.

A real joy in writing these cards is that as I think of each person to whom I am writing wonderful memories are evoked, and it is as if I have spent a day visiting with old friends.

THE HERITAGE BOOK

First Sunday in Advent

OWE nothing to anyone except to love one another, for he who loves his neighbour has fulfilled the law.

—*Romans 13:8*

MONDAY — DECEMBER 4

THE beauty of the world has two edges, one of laughter, one of anguish, cutting the heart asunder.

—*Virginia Woolf*

TUESDAY — DECEMBER 5

IN a drear-nighted December
Too happy, happy tree,
Thy branches ne'er remember
   Their green felicity.

—*John Keats*

IF we had no winter, the spring would not be so pleasant: if we did not sometimes taste of adversity, prosperity would not be so welcome.

—*Anne Bradstreet*

THE HERITAGE BOOK

Chicken Italiano

1-3	pound broiler-fryer, cut up
3	tbsps salad oil
12	garlic cloves
1/2	cup dry white wine
2	tsps salt
1/2	tsp pepper
1/2	tsp dried rosemary leaves
1	medium-sized onion, sliced
4	medium-sized tomatoes, cut into wedges
1	8 oz package spaghetti

coarsely chopped parsley for garnish

Cut each chicken breast half into 2 or 3 pieces. In a 12-inch skillet over medium-high heat, in hot salad oil, cook chicken and garlic until golden brown on all sides, about 20-25 minutes. To chicken and garlic in skillet, add wine, salt, pepper, rosemary, onion and half the tomato wedges; bring to a boil over high heat. Reduce heat to low; cover and simmer 15 minutes or until chicken is fork tender. Skim fat. Add remaining tomatoes; heat through. To serve, drain cooked spaghetti and place on a large platter. Spoon chicken mixture on top and sprinkle with parsley.

Thursday — December 7

Marg and I both enjoyed our volunteer time at school this morning. We helped out in a grade two class as the children worked on Christmas presents for their parents.

The youngsters had a wonderful time decorating their own gingerbread houses. (The "gingerbread" was in fact graham wafers, glued into the form of a small house using an electric glue gun and glue sticks.)

With our help these children constructed their houses. Then, using white icing and a variety of candy, they created homes worthy of the witch's house in the Hansel and Gretel story. Everyone enjoyed sampling the goodies, and happily there were enough sweets to allow each child to both eat and decorate abundantly.

I'm sure that the parents and families who receive these gifts will appreciate the time and effort put into every one.

Friday — December 8

No one is more confusing than the person who gives good advice while setting a bad example.

SATURDAY — DECEMBER 9

IF all the good people were clever,
And all clever people were good,
The world would be nicer than ever
We thought that it possibly could.
—Elizabeth Wordsworth

SUNDAY — DECEMBER 10

Second Sunday in Advent

Now the God of hope fill you with all joy
and peace in believing, that ye may
abound in hope, through the power of the
Holy Ghost.

—Romans 15:13

MONDAY — DECEMBER 11

NOTHING is all wrong. Even a clock that has
stopped running is right twice a day.

THE HERITAGE BOOK

You are not a reservoir with a limited amount of resources; you are a channel attached to unlimited divine resources.

The nursing home in our area offers a daily care program to seniors who do not yet need to live in a Home. This program has been a wonderful help to many local families.

From 8:30 a.m. to 3:30 p.m. a group of fourteen to sixteen elderly people meets in a cheerful area of the Home. During the day they are involved in a number of interesting activities such as crafts, cooking, Bingo, sing-songs, and cards.

A hot nourishing meal is provided at lunchtime and one day a week there is an outing, either a bus trip, a luncheon at a restaurant, or a visit to a museum or theatre.

This program provides a pleasant and stimulating atmosphere and gives the members a chance to form new friendships with peers. And it relieves some of the worry of caring for an elderly parent who is spending day after day alone while the family is at work.

THE HERITAGE BOOK

<u>Thursday — December 14</u>

THE secret of getting things done is to do a little at a time.

<u>Friday — December 15</u>

CHRISTMAS comes but once a year
But when it comes, it brings good cheer.

This proverb certainly proved itself true today. Marg and I spent the afternoon shopping, and in spite of the large numbers of people and the hustle and bustle, everyone I saw had a smile.

<u>Saturday — December 16</u>

I LOVE it, I love it; and who shall dare
To chide me for loving that old armchair?
—*Eliza Cook*

<u>Sunday — December 17</u>

Third Sunday in Advent

I SHALL light a candle of understanding in thine heart, which shall not be put out.
—*Esdras 14:25 The Apocrypha*

THE HERITAGE BOOK

MANY of the young people of our church spent this past weekend in a food collection "blitz." They went from door to door collecting tinned goods, boxed items and, in many cases, money that was pressed upon them by caring neighbours.

The youth group has "adopted" fifteen needy families in our area and is undertaking to provide a happy Christmas Day for them.

The food is being packed in boxes and the money will be spent to buy a turkey with trimmings as well as gifts for the children in each family.

Young people are much criticized today, but when I see these men and women taking time to help others it renews my faith in today's youth.

The greatest reverence is due the young.
—*Juvenal*

THE HERITAGE BOOK

O NE of my favourite activities at this time of year is joining my friends from the seniors group in our annual "Christmas light" bus tour.

Every time we go on this trip I declare that the displays are even lovelier than the year before. This year was no exception. It seemed that in the areas we visited almost every home was decorated in some way. A few houses were modest, having just a few lights on trees or perhaps a door wreath, but many were quite lavish indeed. There were Santas, and reindeer, and one forty-foot pine tree covered in hundreds of coloured bulbs.

My favourite house had a miniature stable scene complete with the creche and Mary and Joseph and the baby Jesus.

After all, He is the "reason for the season."

Wednesday — December 20

I T has the shine of tinsel,
Of crisp and frosty ground,
The very name of Christmas
Has sparkle in its sound.

THURSDAY — DECEMBER 21

THE world is wide; no two days are alike, nor even two hours; neither was there ever two leaves of a tree alike since the creation of the world; and the genuine production of art, like those of nature, are all distinct from each other.

—John Constable

FRIDAY — DECEMBER 22

As Christmas Day approaches one can feel the anticipation in the air. For young children much of the excitement surrounds Santa's visit, but for me it is the chance to have all of our family together again and to enjoy the traditions that span many generations.

This year we have added another activity to the many that we enjoy together. On Christmas Eve all the grandchildren and great-grandchildren will decorate glass balls with their names, the year, and a Christmas design. Each year a different decoration will be chosen and added to the tree.

This is how beautiful memories are made.

SATURDAY — DECEMBER 23

UNTIL one feels the spirit of Christmas, there is no Christmas.

SUNDAY — DECEMBER 24

O LET the nations rejoice and be glad; for thou shalt judge the folk righteously, and govern the nations upon earth.

—Psalm 76:4

MONDAY — DECEMBER 25

Christmas Day

O GOD, who makest us glad with the yearly remembrance of the birth of thy only Son Jesus Christ: Grant that as we joyfully receive him as our Redeemer, we may with sure confidence behold him when he shall come again to be our Judge; who liveth and reigneth with thee and the Holy Ghost now and ever.

—The Common Book of Prayer

TUESDAY — DECEMBER 26

WHAT a wonderful Christmas day we enjoyed! There is nothing that gives me more pleasure than having our whole family together on a happy occasion. We worshipped together at the early service before returning to open the seemingly endless gaily-wrapped packages.

Dinner was a delicious and noisy affair as each of us tried to catch up on days, weeks, or months of news.

It was a day that I will look back on again and again during the coming months.

WEDNESDAY — DECEMBER 27

ANGELS, from the realms of glory
Wing your flight o'er all the earth;
Ye who sang creation's story
Now proclaim Messiah's birth;
Come and worship
Worship Christ, the new born King.

How I love the carols of this season! One of the nicest gifts I received was a tape of Christmas carols and music, which I plan to play throughout the year.

Thursday — December 28

IT'S good to have money and the things that money can buy, but it's good, too, to check up once in a while and make sure that you haven't lost the things that money can't buy.

—*G. H. Lorimer*

Friday — December 29

THERE are two worlds: the world that we can measure with line and rule, and the world that we feel with our heart and imagination.

—*Leigh Hunt*

Saturday — December 30

As the year draws to a close it is enjoyable to sit down and see how many interesting events you can remember from the year nearly past. Marg, Bruce and I did that this evening and we had a good many laughs together.

I hope your joys outnumbered your sorrows and that the year to come will be a happy one for you all.

THE HERITAGE BOOK

Let me live my life from year to year,
With forward face and unreluctant soul;
Not hurrying to, nor turning from, the goal;
Not mourning for the things that disappear
In the dim past, nor holding back in fear
From what the future veils, but with a whole
And happy heart, that pays its toll
To Youth and Age, and travels on with cheer.

So let the way wind up the hill or down,
O'er rough or smooth, the journey will be joy:
Still seeking what I sought when but a boy,
New friendship, high adventure, and a crown,
My heart will keep the courage of the quest,
And hope the road's last turn will be the best.
—Henry Van Dyke

To all my readers, a healthy, happy, and prosperous New Year.